Gifts of Grace

Discovering and Using Your
Spiritual Gifts

Charles Garner and Tony Martin

About the Authors

Charles Garner is an author, curriculum designer, and teacher to the church. His B.A. is in Biblical Studies and Social Science. He holds a Master of Religious Education with emphasis in Biblical Exegesis and Theology.

He has authored, edited, or designed over fifty-five resources and books for use in the Christian community. His works include *Gifts of Grace*, *Developing Deacon-Led Ministry Teams*, *Reclaiming the Real Jesus*, co-authored with Dr. Ivan Parke, *Thinking of Leaving*, *Beyond Expectations*, and *Profiles from Paul*.

He and his wife, Nancy, live in the Northern Rockies of Montana.

Tony Martin, with deep ministry experience in churches across Tennessee, Florida, and Mississippi, has devoted much of his life to writing and editing. He served as Associate Editor of the *Baptist Record*, one of the most widely circulated Christian newspapers in the country. His contribution was pivotal, bringing timely insight and momentum to the work's completion.

Contents

Introduction

"The manifestation of the Spirit is given to each one for the common good... But now God has arranged each one of the members in the body just as He desired... God has so composed the body..."
—1 Corinthians 12:7,18,24

"As each has received a gift, use it to serve one another, as good stewards of God's varied grace."
—1 Peter 4:10

God has given every believer certain spiritual gifts—gifts of grace, expressions of His presence and power at work through us. These grace-gifts equip us to do the ministry He has entrusted to the church. Every Christian has received gifts. Every Christian is a minister. And when we discover and use our gifts, we become more effective, more joyful, and more fruitful in the service of Christ.

Spiritual gifts, however, often stir strong reactions. Some believers fully embrace the concept—finding freedom, focus, and fresh motivation through giftedness. Others are cautious, confused, or even resistant. The mystery that surrounds the gifts—their variety, their power, their sometimes-misunderstood operation—can both attract and unsettle. Unfortunately, some abuses and extremes have left others skeptical or hesitant.

This study seeks to bring clarity and balance. It is grounded in Scripture and shaped by the biblical vision of the church as a gifted, Spirit-empowered Body. Along the way, we'll explore questions like:

- What exactly are spiritual gifts?

- Are talents the same as gifts?

- Are the gifts listed in the Bible the only ones that exist?

- Can gifts be developed?

- When do we receive them?

- How can I discover mine?

- How can we use our gifts without burning out?

- How do gifts shape the ministry of the local church?

God has already given us the greatest gift: salvation through Jesus Christ. He has also commissioned us for ministry in His name. And—true to His character—He has not left us unequipped. Spiritual gifts are the divine resources for the divine calling.

As you begin this journey, pray that God will help you see more clearly the gifts He has placed in your life—and the ministry He is preparing for you in and through the Body of Christ.

To the Corinthians
—a word about spiritual gifts—

1 Now concerning spiritual gifts, brethren, I would not have you ignorant. 2 Ye know that ye were Gentiles, carried away unto these dumb idols, even as ye were led. 3 Wherefore I give you to understand, that no man speaking by the Spirit of God calleth Jesus accursed: and that no man can say that Jesus is the Lord, but by the Holy Ghost.

4 Now there are diversities of gifts, but the same Spirit.

5 And there are differences of administrations, but the same Lord.

6 And there are diversities of operations, but it is the same God which worketh all in all.

7 But the manifestation of the Spirit is given to every man to profit withal.

8 For to one is given by the Spirit the word of wisdom; to another the word of knowledge by the same Spirit; 9 To another faith by the same Spirit; to another the gifts of healing by the same Spirit; 10 To another the working of miracles; to another prophecy; to another discerning of spirits; to another divers kinds of tongues; to another the interpretation of tongues:

11 But all these worketh that one and the selfsame Spirit, dividing to every man severally as he will. 12 But as the body is one, and hath many members, and all the members of that body, being many, are one body: so also is Christ.

13 For by one Spirit are we all baptized into one body, whether we be Jews or Gentiles, whether we be bond or free; and have been all made to drink into one Spirit.

—1 Corinthians 12:1-13

Session 1
The Inventory

Directions: Take the inventory at this time. The *Spiritual Gifts Inventory*[1] will aid you in discovering and understanding your spiritual gifts. Your honest thoughtful response to the inventory will help in obtaining the best results. You will be given instructions for scoring and interpreting the inventory later.

Your response choices are:
5 - Highly characteristic

4 - Most of the time

3 - Frequently

2 - Occasionally

1 - Not at all

Before you begin—just a few comments...
This is not a test, so *there are no wrong answers*. The inventory consists of 103 items. Some of these reflect concrete actions; others are descriptive traits; and still others are statements of belief. You are asked to indicate how descriptive the item is of you.

Record your response by placing in the blank beside each item the number which corresponds to the answer you want.

Do not spend too much time on any one item. Remember, it's not a test. Mark the extent to which you feel the item is descriptive of you. Usually your immediate response is best.

Please give a response for *each item*. Do not skip any items.

Work at your own pace.

Spiritual Gifts Inventory

_____ 1. I have the ability to organize ideas, resources, time, and people effectively.

_____ 2. I am willing to study and prepare for the task of teaching.

_____ 3. I am able to relate the truths of God to specific situations.

_____ 4. I inspire persons to right actions by pointing out the blessings of this path.

_____ 5. I have a God-given ability to help others grow in their faith.

_____ 6. I possess a special ability to communicate the truth of salvation.

_____ 7. I am sensitive to the hurts of people.

_____ 8. I experience joy in meeting needs through sharing possessions.

_____ 9. I enjoy study.

_____ 10. I have delivered God's messages of warning and judgment.

_____ 11. I am able to sense the true motivations of persons and movements.

_____ 12. I trust God in difficult situations.

_____ 13. I have a strong desire to contribute to the establishment of new churches.

_____ 14. I feel God has used me in a supernatural event.

_____ 15. I enjoy doing things for people in need.

_____ 16. I am aware of a special appropriation of God's healing power through myself.

_____ 17. I have been moved to express such intense spiritual feelings that what came from my mouth was unintelligible to most people.

_____ 18. Words or thoughts come to me in an inspiring way after a message in an unknown language is delivered in group worship.

_____ 19. I can delegate and assign meaningful work.

_____ 20. I have an ability and desire to teach.

_____ 21. I am usually able to analyze a situation correctly.

_____ 22. I have a tendency to encourage and reward others.

_____ 23. I am willing to take the initiative in helping other Christians grow in their faith.

_____ 24. I am unafraid to share with lost people.

_____ 25. I have an acute awareness of such emotions as loneliness, pain, fear, and anger in others.

_____ 26. I am a cheerful giver.

_____ 27. I spend time digging into facts.

_____ 28. I feel that I have a message from God to deliver to others.

_____ 29. I can recognize when a person is genuine/honest.

_____ 30. I am willing to yield to God's will rather than question and waver.

_____ 31. I would like to be more active in getting the gospel to people in other lands.

_____ 32. I have been used by God to bring about supernatural changes.

_____ 33. It makes me happy to do things for people in need.

_____ 34. I am willing to be an instrument of healing.

_____ 35. I have had an awareness of wanting to praise God in utterances which one's heart feels but which one's mind does not understand.

_____ 36. I have prayed that I may interpret if someone begins speaking in tongues.

_____ 37. I am successful in getting a group to do its work joyfully.

_____ 38. I have the ability to plan learning approaches.

_____ 39. I have been able to offer solutions to spiritual problems others are facing.

_____ 40. I can identify those who need encouragement.

_____ 41. I have trained Christians to be more obedient disciples of Christ.

_____ 42. I am willing to do whatever it takes to see others come to Christ.

_____ 43. I am attracted to people who are hurting.

_____ 44. I am a generous giver.

_____ 45. I am able to discover new truths.

_____ 46. I have spiritual insights from Scripture concerning issues and people which compel me to speak out.

_____ 47. I can sense when a person is acting in accord with God's will.

_____ 48. I can trust God even when things look dark.

_____ 49. I have a strong desire to take the gospel to places where it has never been heard.

_____ 50. I have been used by God to accomplish a miracle.

_____ 51. I enjoy helping people.

_____ 52. I understand scriptural teachings regarding healing.

_____ 53. I believe that speaking in tongues may be edifying to the Lord's Body.

_____ 54. I am able to interpret the ecstatic utterances of others.

_____ 55. I have been able to make effective and efficient plans for accomplishing the goals of a group.

_____ 56. I understand the variety of ways people learn.

_____ 57. I am often consulted when fellow Christians are struggling to make difficult decisions.

_____ 58. I think about how I can comfort and encourage others in my congregation.

_____ 59. I am able to give spiritual direction to others.

_____ 60. I am able to present the gospel to lost persons in such a way that they accept the Lord and His salvation.

_____ 61. I possess an unusual capacity to understand the feelings of those in distress.

_____ 62. I have a strong sense of stewardship based on the recognition of God's ownership of all things.

_____ 63. I know where to get information.

_____ 64. I have delivered to other persons messages which have come directly from God.

_____ 65. I can sense when a person is acting under God's leadership.

_____ 66. I try to be continually in God's will.

_____ 67. I feel I should take the gospel to people who have different beliefs from me.

_____ 68. I have been God's instrument to bring about supernatural change in lives or events.

_____ 69. I love to do things for people.

_____ 70. I am aware of the miraculous aspects of life.

_____ 71. I enjoy being with persons who speak in tongues.

_____ 72. I have prayed that I may be able to interpret tongues.

_____ 73. I am skilled in setting forth positive and precise steps of action.

_____ 74. I explain Scripture in such a way that others understand it.

_____ 75. I can usually see spiritual solutions to problems.

_____ 76. I am glad when people who need comfort, consolation, encouragement, and counsel seek my help.

_____ 77. I am able to nurture others.

_____ 78. I feel at ease in sharing Christ with nonbelievers.

_____ 79. I recognize the signs of stress and distress in others.

_____ 80. I desire to give generously and unpretentiously to worthwhile projects and ministries.

_____ 81. I can organize facts into meaningful relationships.

_____ 82. God gives me messages to deliver to His people.

_____ 83. I am able to sense whether people are being honest when they tell of their religious experiences.

_____ 84. I try to be available for God to use.

_____ 85. I enjoy presenting the gospel to persons of other cultures and backgrounds.

_____ 86. I have been used by God to bring about a powerful act which could not be explained in human terms.

_____ 87. I enjoy doing little things that help people.

_____ 88. I am aware of the supernatural power at work within my life.

_____ 89. Speaking in tongues enables me to be more effective in all areas of my life.

_____ 90. I can plan a strategy and "bring others aboard."

_____ 91. I can give a clear, uncomplicated presentation.

_____ 92. I have been able to apply biblical truth to the specific needs of my church.

_____ 93. God has used me to encourage others to live Christ-like lives.

_____ 94. I have sensed the need to help other people become more effective in their ministries.

_____ 95. I like to talk about Jesus to those who do not know Him.

_____ 96. I feel assured that a situation will change for the glory of God even when the situation seems impossible.

_____ 97. I am able to nurture others.

_____ 98. I have an awareness that God still heals people as He did in biblical times.

_____ 99. I have matured in my spiritual life as a result of speaking in tongues.

_____ 100. I sense God's intervention in events.

_____101. I have witnessed miraculous answers to my prayers.

_____102. I believe God can and does act in miraculous ways.

_____103. I have a burning desire to see people who are suffering be made well.

Now...score yourself.

On the next page you will find the scoring instrument. Follow these instructions:

1. For each gift place in the boxes the number of the response you gave for each item indicated below the box.
2. For each gift add the numbers in the boxes and put the total (sum) in the "TOTAL" box.
3. For each gift divide the TOTAL by the number indicated and place the result in the "SCORE" box (round each answer to one decimal place, such as 3.7). This is your score for the gift.

Gift   (Hint: score more quickly, fill the boxes vertically)

Leadership

☐ + ☐ + ☐ + ☐ + ☐ +
Item 1   Item 19   Item 37   Item 55   Item 73

☐ = ☐ ÷ 6 = ☐
Item 90   TOTAL   SCORE

Teaching

☐ + ☐ + ☐ + ☐ + ☐ +
Item 2   Item 20   Item 38   Item 56   Item 74

☐ = ☐ ÷ 6 = ☐
Item 91   TOTAL   SCORE

Knowledge

☐ + ☐ + ☐ + ☐ + ☐ +
Item 9   Item 27   Item 45   Item 63   Item 81

☐ = ☐ ÷ 6 = ☐
Item 96   TOTAL   SCORE

Wisdom

☐ + ☐ + ☐ + ☐ + ☐ +
Item 3   Item 21   Item 39   Item 57   Item 75

☐ = ☐ ÷ 6 = ☐
Item 92   TOTAL   SCORE

Prophecy

☐ + ☐ + ☐ + ☐ + ☐ =
Item 4   Item 22   Item 40   Item 58   Item 76

☐ ÷ 5 = ☐
TOTAL   SCORE

Spiritual Discernment

☐ + ☐ + ☐ + ☐ + ☐ =
Item 11   Item 29   Item 47   Item 65   Item 83

☐ ÷ 5 − ☐
TOTAL   SCORE

Encouragement

☐ + ☐ + ☐ + ☐ + ☐ +
Item 4   Item 22   Item 40   Item 58   Item 76

☐ = ☐ ÷ 6 = ☐
Item 93   TOTAL   SCORE

Shepherding   [ ] Item 5 + [ ] Item 23 + [ ] Item 41 + [ ] Item 59 + [ ] Item 77 +

[ ] Item 94 = [ ] TOTAL ÷ 6 = [ ] SCORE

Faith   [ ] Item 12 + [ ] Item 30 + [ ] Item 48 + [ ] Item 66 + [ ] Item 84 +

[ ] Item 97 = [ ] TOTAL ÷ 6 = [ ] SCORE

Evangelism   [ ] Item 6 + [ ] Item 24 + [ ] Item 42 + [ ] Item 60 + [ ] Item 78 +

[ ] Item 95 = [ ] TOTAL ÷ 6 = [ ] SCORE

Apostleship   [ ] Item 13 + [ ] Item 31 + [ ] Item 49 + [ ] Item 67 + [ ] Item 85 =

[ ] TOTAL ÷ 5 = [ ] SCORE

Miracles   [ ] Item 14 + [ ] Item 32 + [ ] Item 50 + [ ] Item 68 + [ ] Item 86 =

[ ] TOTAL ÷ 5 = [ ] SCORE

Helps   [ ] Item 15 + [ ] Item 33 + [ ] Item 51 + [ ] Item 69 + [ ] Item 87 =

[ ] TOTAL ÷ 5 = [ ] SCORE

Mercy   [ ] Item 7 + [ ] Item 25 + [ ] Item 43 + [ ] Item 61 + [ ] Item 79 =

[ ] TOTAL ÷ 5 = [ ] SCORE

Giving

☐ + ☐ + ☐ + ☐ + ☐ =
Item 8   Item 26   Item 44   Item 62   Item 80

☐ ÷ 5 = ☐
TOTAL   **SCORE**

Healing

☐ + ☐ + ☐ + ☐ + ☐ +
Item 16   Item 34   Item 52   Item 70   Item 88

☐ + ☐ + ☐ + ☐ + ☐ =
Item 98   Item 101   Item 100   Item 102   Item 103

☐ ÷ 10 = ☐
TOTAL   **SCORE**

Tongues

☐ + ☐ + ☐ + ☐ + ☐ +
Item 17   Item 35   Item 53   Item 71   Item 89

☐ = ☐ ÷ 6 = ☐
Item 99   TOTAL   **SCORE**

Interpretation

☐ + ☐ + ☐ + ☐ =
Item 18   Item 36   Item 54   Item 72

☐ ÷ 4 = ☐
TOTAL   **SCORE**

Graphing Your Profile

1. For each gift, draw a line across the bar for that gift at the point which corresponds to your SCORE for that gift.
2. For each gift, shade the bar below the line which you have drawn.
3. The resultant graph gives a "picture" of your gifts. The higher the shaded bar, the stronger the gift is in your life. The combination of these strong gifts might provide an indication of the ministry for which God has gifted you.

	Leadership	Teaching	Knowledge	Wisdom	Prophecy	Spiritual Discernment	Encouragement	Shepherding	Faith	Evangelism	Apostleship	Miracles	Helps	Mercy	Giving	Healing	Tongues	Interpretation
5.0																		
4.0																		
3.0																		
2.0																		
1.0																		
0.0																		

Grace Gifted
Definitions/Explanations
of Spiritual Gifts

Throughout this section of definitions/explanations you will have opportunity to write your own working definition of the various gifts. Read the definitions provided, read the passages of Scripture to see how the gifts were used in the early church, and then write your own definition in the space provided.

Leadership/Administration/Government
To set or place over. To be over, to superintend, preside over. To be a protector or guardian, to give aid.
Thayer's Greek-English Lexicon of the New Testament (p. 539)

To guide, as in piloting a ship.
Vines Expository Dictionary of New Testament Words (p. 508)

The ability to direct and guide a church with wise counsel in conducting the ministry God has given.
Spiritual Gifts Inventory (BSSB, unpublished)

See Acts 6:1-8; Titus 1:5; Acts 15:1-31.

Teaching
The special ability to study God's word and to communicate spiritual truths in such a way that they are relevant to the health and ministry of the church and in a way that others will learn.
Spiritual Gifts Inventory

See Acts 11:22-26.

Knowledge

The ability to discover, understand, clarify, and communicate information that relates to the life, growth, and well-being of the church. *Spiritual Gifts Inventory*

The deeper, more perfect and enlarged knowledge of this religion, such as belongs to the more advanced. *Thayer (p.119)*

To come to know, recognize, understand, or to understand completely. *Vines (p. 637)*

See Acts 18:24-28.

Wisdom

Broad and full intelligence, used of the knowledge of very diverse matters. The ability to discourse eloquently of this wisdom. *Thayer (p. 582)*

The ability to gain insight into the practical application of God's truth to specific situations. *Spiritual Gifts Inventory*

The practical application of insight into divine wisdom to our own and to others' lives. *The Interpretation of 1 and 2 Corinthians*, Lenski (p. 500)

See Acts 15:1-31.

Prophecy/Prophet

One who speaks forth the word of God. The proclaimer of a divine message. The purpose of this ministry is to edify, to comfort, to encourage the believers (1 Cor. 14:3). Prophecy's effect upon unbelievers was to show that the secrets of a person's heart are known to God, to convict of sin, and to constrain to worship (1 Cor. 14:24-25). *Vines (p. 903)*

The special ability to receive from God a message and then to communicate that message to others through a divinely anointed utterance. *Spiritual Gifts Inventory*

See Acts 11:27-30.

Spiritual Discernment

The ability to discriminate between that which is of the Holy Spirit and that which is not, especially as it pertains to oral testimony. *Vines (p. 317)*

The ability to know which actions and teachings that are claimed to be of God are actually of God (and not human or satanic). *Spiritual Gifts Inventory*

See 1 John 5:1.

Encouragement

The special ability to comfort and encourage others as well as to motivate others to right actions. *Spiritual Gifts Inventory*

To stand alongside another giving support and comfort—to console, to give aid to another. *Vines*

To address, speak to, which may be done in the way of exhortation, entreaty, comfort, instruction—hence encouragement embraces a variety of senses.

See Acts 4:31-37; 9:26-27.

Shepherding/Pastor
Tending herds or flocks—giving tender care and vigilant supervision. *Vines (p. 849)*

The overseers of Christian assemblies. *Thayer (p. 527)*

Exercising care and control over others. The ability to build up, equip, and guide Christians toward spiritual maturity. *Spiritual Gifts Inventory*

See 1 Peter 5:1-4; Ephesians 4:11-16.

Faith
The special ability to discern and affirm God's will and purposes in the world and to be a part of His intervention through prayer and the Spirit's power. *Spiritual Gifts Inventory*

The supernatural ability to perceive the will of God and to commit one's self to doing it.

See Acts 8:26-40.

Evangelism/Evangelist
A messenger of good. A preacher of the gospel. *Vines (p. 384)*

The ability to comprehend the lost condition of people in the world and to present Christ effectively so that persons will accept salvation in Jesus. *Spiritual Gifts Inventory*

See Acts 8:4ff.

Apostleship/Apostle

A sending, a mission. One sent on a mission. *Thayer (p. 65)*

The ability to share the gospel in special ways. These are persons who are sent by God with His message of reconciliation. *Spiritual Gifts Inventory*

See Acts 9:1-22.

Miracles

Power, inherent ability, used of works of a supernatural origin and character, such as could not be produced by natural agents and means. *Vines (p.757)*

The special ability to serve as human intermediaries through which God works to bring about events that cannot be explained by natural law. *Spiritual Gifts Inventory*

See Acts 19:11-12.

Helps/Service

Abilities for rendering helpful services to the destitute, the sick, the persecuted, the troubled. Services for the sake of services. *The Interpretation of 1 and 2 Corinthians*, Lenski (p. 540)

The ability to render service to benefit and help others, this being the only motive—all compulsion being absent. Helpful, voluntary service motivated by obedience to God as a servant.

The ability and desire to recognize day-to-day needs of others and to meet those needs personally. *Spiritual Gifts Inventory*

Assistance rendered, especially to the weak and needy. *Vines (p. 317)*

The ministrations of the deacons who have care of the poor and the sick. *Thayer (p. 50)*

See Acts 6:1-8; Philippians 2:25-30.

Mercy
The outward manifestation of pity. Mercy is the act of God on behalf of needy persons. *Vines (p. 742)*

The merciful person is to greet every opportunity for a merciful deed as a great find that makes him jubilant. Grudging mercy is not to be his manner of doing. We are to show mercy with great joy (literally, hilarity). *Romans*, Lenski (p. 765)

Kindness or good will toward the miserable and afflicted, joined with a desire to relieve them. *Thayer (p. 203)*

The ability to feel sympathy and compassion for and to meet actively the needs of persons who suffer distress and crises from the physical, mental, emotional problems. *Spiritual Gifts Inventory*

See Acts 9:36.

Giving

To give a share of, to impart (meta, with), as distinct from giving. The sense means to do more than to give one's physical or material goods. It encompasses that, but moves beyond it to indicate a sharing with others so as to spend or pour out one's life for others. Paul used this term in Romans 1:11 when he wrote that he wanted to see the Roman Christians so he could impart (give) some spiritual gift to them. He did not mean that he would give them a gift, but rather, that he would share or impart his gift or gifts for their benefit. *Vines (p. 489)*

To share a thing with anyone. *Thayer (p. 404)*

The ability and desire to contribute material resources to others and the Lord's work with liberality and cheerfulness. *Spiritual Gifts Inventory*

See Acts 4:36-37; Romans 1:11.

Healing

Divinely imparted gifts of physical and spiritual healing. Carries with it the concept of wholeness, being made whole. *Vines (p.543-544)*

The God-given ability to help others regain physical, mental, or spiritual health through the direct action of God. *Spiritual Gifts Inventory*

See Acts 16:16-18.

Tongues

The special ability to speak to God through Spirit-inspired utterances and/or to receive and communicate an immediate message of God to His people through Spirit-inspired utterances.
Spiritual Gifts Inventory

The supernatural gift of speaking in another language without having learned it. *Vines (p. 1165)*

Language spoken by persons who in rapt ecstasy are no longer quite masters of their own reason and consciousness. They pour forth their glowing spiritual emotions in strange utterances, rugged, dark, disconnected, quite unfitted to instruct or to influence the minds of others. *Thayer (p. 188)*

See Acts 10:44-48 and Acts 19:1-7.

Interpretation

To unfold the meaning of what is said, explain, expound.
Thayer (p. 147)

The conversion of what is unintelligible into what is intelligible.
Theological Dictionary of the New Testament (p. 665)

The ability to convey a rational account of what was spoken in a tongue. *The Interpreter's Dictionary of the Bible* (p. 672)

[Although the gift of interpretation is mentioned, no specific instance of the gift is given in the text of the New Testament. Some think that the explanation offered by Peter (Acts 2:13ff.) on the Day of Pentecost was interpretation.]

Session 2
You Have *Charisma*!

In 1978 the Personnel Committee of the Mississippi Baptist Convention Board requested the presence of a young man they were considering for a position on their staff. The man was on staff of one of the churches in the state. The question/answer period went well. All questions had been answered to everyone's satisfaction. The atmosphere was positive. Apparently, the situation was moving toward an agreeable resolution.

The chairman of the committee, a prominent pastor in the state, began speaking about the trouble he was having in his church and association with "tongues speakers." He then bluntly and unexpectedly asked the candidate, "Are you charismatic?"

The entire committee focused attention on the young man. Nobody had to tell him that a critical moment had arrived. His career flashed before him as he considered his response.

 **In the place of the young man, how would you have responded?**

 Several years ago Emily Andreano wrote an article about the late news anchorman, Peter Jennings, entitled *"Charismatic Correspondent."* What do you think Andreano meant by *charismatic*?

Write your response here.

Many people are described as *charismatic*. Usually when this term is applied to persons outside certain religious circles, it means they have a certain appeal or presence about them. They seem to draw people by an inner force. This force might result from a variety of factors—physical appearance, voice, stature, bearing, mental acumen—whatever the factors, these people have *charisma*.

Instructions: Indicate the level of response (positive/negative) on the following scale toward the word *charisma* as used in the title of the article about Peter Jennings by circling a number on the scale.

Negative										Positive
-5	-4	-3	-2	-1	0	+1	+2	+3	+4	+5

Pardon me while I date myself…

I was that young man being interviewed in 1978. Just three years earlier, an article appeared in nation-wide stories proclaiming that speaking in tongues was of the devil. The article was targeted at "charismatics." None other than Dr. W. A. Criswell, pastor of the historic First Baptist Church of Dallas, Texas, made that statement.

So my career did flash in front of my eyes when confronted by the chairman's question, "Are you charismatic?" I knew my answer would determine to an extent my future opportunities for service.

Especially in Southern Baptist circles. I was just 28 years of age. In the boardroom of a prestigious Christian organization composed of over 2300 churches. Talk about a pressure moment. I felt heat.

Peter Jennings, the head of ABC News, was a "charismatic" figure. His career spanned the globe. He was esteemed as a top journalist. He was described as a bright star, dynamic person, charismatic, energetic, a man of elegance and grace, a man who could command a room. The accolades and praise are almost endless.

How can it be that one use of the word, *charismatic*, is applauded in one context and strikes near-panic in another? We will explore this contrast to get to a degree of truth about one of the more central tenets of faith in Christian experience.

Oh, and I did get that position with the Mississippi Baptist Convention in 1978. Because I knew the Scripture.

The worship services at Bethany Fellowship are quite different than those of Calvary Lutheran Church. Often the services are marked by exuberant singing and hand waving from the congregation, members speaking randomly, and some persons speaking in tongues. Occasionally, they will have a healing service in which people go forward for the church leaders to lay hands on them. These people are known as "charismatics."

Instructions: Indicate the level of response (positive/negative) on the following scale toward the word *charismatic* as used in this account by circling a number on the scale.

Negative										Positive
-5	-4	-3	-2	-1	0	+1	+2	+3	+4	+5

Usually, we respond positively to the use of charismatic when it refers to an individual having a sense of presence, power, and personal appeal, as in the case of the article about Peter Jennings. However, the same word, when applied to religious expression, causes a negative reaction in many. Why? Sometimes the negative response is due to fear of abuses of spiritual gifts, fear of disruption in churches, fear of an experience outside the range of personal experience, and even a theological bias against the relevance of spiritual gifts today.

Many of these issues will be explored further in the additional sessions of this study. Let's begin our exploration of spiritual gifts with a look at the word *charismatic*.

> **Editor's note:** Some segments of this study look at the original language of the New Testament text. No extensive or prior knowledge of the Greek language is required to work through the passages. Use these as visual illustrations if the language is distracting. However, it is often necessary to look at the original languages to gain a true biblical perspective on an issue or doctrine.

Spiritual Gifts or Gifts of Grace?

The term "spiritual" gifts is actually somewhat of a misnomer. The word translated as spiritual gifts is *pneumatikon*. Paul used this word generally to indicate or describe the condition of being spiritual. Only in three or four references in his writings did Paul use this word to indicate spiritual gifts. In the context of 1 Corinthians 12:1, the word lends itself to mean spiritual gifts: *Now concerning spiritual gifts (pneumatikon) brethren, I would not have you ignorant.*

Pneumatikon refers to things emanating from the Holy Spirit, produced by the sole power of God Himself without natural instrumentality (Thayer). Most translators use the phrase, spiritual gifts, to interpret the meaning of Paul in 1 Corinthians 12:1. These gifts are "spiritual" in that they are given by the Holy Spirit (1 Cor. 12:7, 11) and are given to be used in our spiritual ministries.

In most instances, when referring to the gifts of the Spirit, the writers of the New Testament used the words *charisma* (gift) or *charismata* (gifts). [See Rms. 12:6; 1 Cor. 7:7; 12:4, 9, 30, 31; 1 Peter 4:10.] The base of these phrases is *charis*—the word for grace. Grace is the unmerited favor of God. Rather than referring always to spiritual gifts, at times a more accurate understanding or translation would be grace gift or grace gifts. Interestingly, the root word for *charis* is *char*—meaning joy. God's saving grace and His grace gifts are the sources of joy in the believer's life.

Spiritual gifts or grace gifts are addressed extensively by Paul in his first letter to the Corinthians (1 Cor. 12-14). This is the largest section in the New Testament dealing with spiritual gifts.

Paul and the Corinthian Problems

This passage is part of Paul's response to a letter from the Corinthians in which they asked Paul about several specific issues. This larger section begins in 1 Corinthians 7:1—*Now concerning the matters about which you wrote*....

The questions raised by the Corinthians appear to concern:
-marital relationships (7:1b-40)
-food offered to idols (8:1-11:1)
-the practices of public worship (11:2-14:40)
-the role of women in worship (11:2-16)
-the Lord's supper (11:17-34)
-spiritual gifts (12:1-14:40)
-the resurrection (15:1-58)
-the collection for the saints (16:1-4)

Paul addressed the question of spiritual gifts in 1 Corinthians 12:1-14:40. This section forms the largest section in the New Testament devoted to spiritual gifts and their function in the church.

The foundational assumption behind this passage is that the practice of speaking in tongues was being promoted in the Corinthian church as a matter of common practice. In addition, we gain the sense that a "spiritual" hierarchy had developed around this particular practice. Those who spoke in tongues apparently looked down upon those who did not speak with tongues. Seemingly, the gift of tongues had become an expectation for all the Corinthian believers.

Paul's response to the question about spiritual gifts includes three distinct sections:

- theological foundations (12:1-31)
- the ruling ethic (13:1-3)
- practical instructions (14:1-40)

This large passage, along with others in the New Testament, will be explored in several of our study sessions. You might feel the desire to deal with all of these immediately. That's normal. Just remember that spiritual gifts is a complex issue. Be patient. We will deal with the whole in digestible bites.

One of the issues Paul addressed in 1 Corinthians (12:1-14:40) was the mistaken idea that all believers were to possess any one of the gifts. Paul went immediately to the point of error at the beginning of chapter 12 where he asserted that there are diversities of gifts (12:4). The theme continued at the end of the chapter where Paul asked a series of rhetorical questions (1 Cor. 12:29-30) aimed at showing that all do not possess the same gift or gifts.

Paul's opening statements affirm the common or universal role of the Holy Spirit in salvation (1 Cor. 12:2-3). Every believer comes to Christ drawn by the Holy Spirit. Paul then immediately began a series of statements about the diversities of God's work in individual Christian lives. While no clear definition of a spiritual or grace gift is provided in the New Testament, in his statements about God's various expressions and workings in Christians' lives, Paul provided us with an idea of what a spiritual gift is: *Now there are diversities of gifts, but the same Spirit. And there are differences of administrations, but the same Lord. And there are diversities of operations, but it is the same God which worketh all in all. But the manifestation of the Spirit is given to every man to profit withal* (1 Cor. 12:4-7).

What Is a Spiritual Gift?

In this passage, four different words are used by Paul that reveal insights into spiritual gifts. Paul used the words gifts (v. 4), administrations (v. 5), operations (v.6), and manifestation (v.7) in addressing the idea of spiritual gifts. As a facetted diamond held up to the light glows with various colors as the light is diffracted, we see various aspects or dimensions to spiritual gifts as with each verse another facet is turned to the light. These words, taken as a composite, provide a sense of what is meant by spiritual gift.

Look at the following passage from an interlinear Greek New Testament[1] to see the various words used by Paul. [Remember that you do not need to be a scholar, just a good student. Look at the highlighted words. This text is simply for awareness of what Paul wrote.]

ματι ἁγίῳ. 4 διαιρέσεις.δὲ (χαρισμάτων) εἰσίν. τὸ.δὲ αὐτὸ
  [1]Holy.   But diversities   of gifts   there are, but the same
πνεῦμα· 5 καὶ διαιρέσεις(διακονιῶν) εἰσίν, καὶ ὁ αὐτὸς κύριος·
  Spirit ;   and diversities   of services there are, and the same   Lord ;
6 καὶ διαιρέσεις(ἐνεργημάτων) εἰσίν, ἰ.ὁ.δὲ αὐτὸς ἰἐστιν[II] θεός,
  and diversities   of operations   there are, but the same   [2]it [3]is   [1]God,
ὁ ἐνεργῶν τὰ.πάντα ἐν πᾶσιν. 7 ἑκάστῳ.δὲ δίδοται ἡ(φανέ-
who operates all things   in   all.   But to each   is given the mani-
ρωσις) τοῦ πνεύματος πρὸς τὸ συμφέρον. 8 ᾧ.μὲν.γὰρ διὰ
festation of the   Spirit   for   profit.   For to one   by

Note these four words on the following chart—

Verse 4	χαρισμάτων	> *charismaton* = grace gifts
Verse 5	διακονίων	> *diakonion* = service/ministry
Verse 6	ἐνεργημάτων	> *energamaton* = empowerings/ workings
Verse 7	φανέρωσις	> *phanerosis* = revealing/ manifestation

In each verse, Paul used a different word referring to God's activity in the lives of believers. In 12:4, Paul used the word *charismaton*, a plural form translated as grace gifts. He emphasized the universality of the Spirit, but the diversity of gifts. In 12:5, he used the word *diakonion*, a word meaning ministries or services. He emphasized the diversity of ministries while pointing to the universality of the Lord. In 12:6, Paul emphasized the diversities of the workings, operations or empowerings by using *energamaton*, while emphasizing the universality of God. In 12:7, Paul used a completely different word, *phanerosis*, meaning a revealing or a manifestation, in referring to the phenomenon of the Holy Spirit's work in our lives.

Read these verses—1 Corinthians 12:4-7. Look at the four words on the chart. Using these four words, compose your own definition of a spiritual gift.

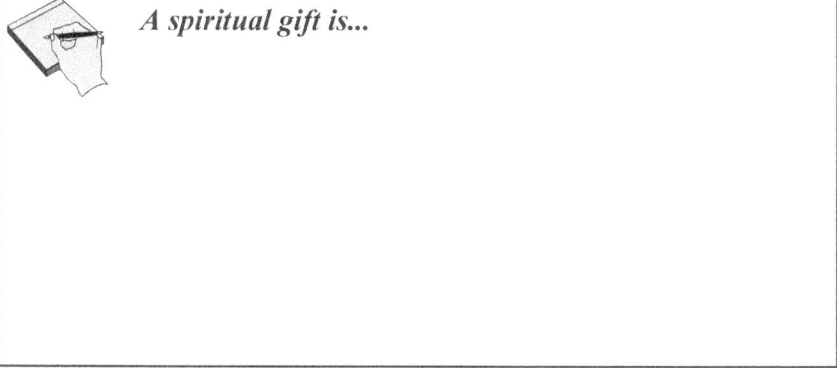

A spiritual gift is...

Each word in these verses reveals a different facet of spiritual gifts. Combining them, we gain an understanding of what Paul meant by *spiritual gift*.

A *spiritual gift* is a supernatural ability given by grace empowering believers for service and displaying the presence of God in our lives.

Spiritual Gifts, Talents, and Skills

What's the difference between a spiritual gift, a natural talent, and a skill? Aren't they all the same? The short answer is—no, they are not the same.

A *spiritual gift* is a supernatural evidence of God's presence in a Christian's life. Spiritual gifts are special abilities given to empower us for the service or ministry that God has given us to do in and through the Body of Christ, the church. Spiritual gifts come as a result of a spiritual birth. (It is unclear exactly when these gifts are given—at the salvation experience or as they are needed by the church. God could do either. <u>When</u> is not nearly so important as the fact that they are given.)

A *talent* is a natural ability resulting from a natural birth. A talent is a result of the combination of muscle, bone, sinew, neurons, and other factors composing our natural bodies.

A *skill* is merely the learned application of spiritual gifts or natural talents.

 **Explain in your own words the difference between a spiritual gift, a talent, and a skill.**

Are You Charismatic?

Are you charismatic? Yes, you are if you are a Christian. The word charismatic is based on *charis*, a word translated as <u>grace</u>. Grace is the unmerited favor of God. *Charismatic* means one is grace-gifted.

God in His grace has given us a variety of gifts—one of those gifts is salvation. The New Testament affirms that believers in Jesus Christ are saved by God's grace. Paul stated this throughout his letters, but never more clearly than in his letter to the Ephesian Christians—*For by grace are ye saved through faith; and that not of yourselves: it is the gift of God: not of works, lest any man should boast* (Eph. 2:8-9). Because believers have received the gift of God's grace, we are <u>charismatic</u>. God has gifted us for *salvation*.

God has also gifted us for *service*. As believers, we have all been commissioned to ministry, to service. God never commands us to do something without providing the necessary resources to do the work He has given us to do. Peter instructs us that every believer has been given a gift (or gifts) essential to the ministry that God has called us to do—*As every man hath received the gift, even so minister the same to one another, as good stewards of the manifold grace of God* (1 Peter 4:10).

A recent popular movement within the Christian community has so redefined the word and ideas behind *charismatic* that many Christians reject the word when applied to them. Rather than rejecting the concept of being charismatic, we need to define (or redefine in some instances) the concept. Being charismatic is not just a perfectly good biblical concept, but one that is absolutely essential to our doing the ministry God has called us to do.

The grace gifts of God are essential to salvation and to service. The grace gifts are foundational to the very idea of being Christian. Every believer has received God's gifts of grace—for salvation and for service— and is charismatic because of those gifts.

When confronted by the chairman of the Personnel Committee, I did see my career flashing in front of me and going down the drain. After considering my potential responses, I replied, "Yes, I'm charismatic and so are you." Then, I went on to reply to his question with the essential word study we have just covered.

The chairman was responding to a situation in contemporary church life in the 1970's. He probably expected a simple denial that I was "charismatic." He, nor, the Committee expected the answer they received. I had taken my stance on the truth of Scripture. On the exact meaning of the word and the subsequent doctrine.

You could have heard the proverbial pin drop when I finished.

The silence was broken by Dr. Brooks Wester, pastor of First Baptist Church of Hattiesburg. Dr. Wester sat at the opposite end of the conference table from the chairman. He slapped the table and spoke to the Committee, "Let's hire this boy before someone else gets him."

Truth had been stated. Dr. Wester, an excellent biblical scholar himself, recognized it. And moved the Committee to employ me. That was a turning point in my journey in service. Other doors of opportunity were opened in years yet to come because a biblical position had been taken.

And that is what we are wanting. We want to know what God has said about His gifts of grace that He invests into our lives for the ministries to which He calls us.

 After church one recent Sunday, Les and Jeanette Elam were at lunch with some friends. The conversation turned to a particular church in the community known as a "charismatic" church.

The Elams' friends were Christians—had been for many years. Jack told Les, "I've been a Christian a long time, but I'm not charismatic."

Les had been attending a spiritual gifts seminar offered at his church. He had studied what it means to be truly charismatic.

Put yourself in Les' place. How would you respond to Jack?

Notes and Observations

Session 3
Why Are the Gifts Given?

In John 14 is one of the more astounding verses in all the Bible.

Verily, verily, I say unto you, He that believeth on me, the works that I do shall he do also; and greater works than these shall he do; because I go unto my Father (John 14:12 KJV).

 **With your Bible open to John 14:12, complete the following questions**:

What is the context of this statement? Where was Jesus when He said this? What prompted Jesus to say this?

What do you think Jesus meant? What are the things Jesus did?

How did Jesus do the things He did? (See Matt. 12:28 and John 14:10.)

What is the primary subject of the teaching that follows this statement? (Note John 14:16-17. Also, note what Jesus said in 14:18 and in 14:23 about His and the Father's relationship to His followers.)

What did Jesus say we could do in our own energy, intellect, and resources? (Note John 15:5.)

Why were the disciples told to wait in Jerusalem (Acts 1:4)? (See Acts 1:5, 8.)

Why can't we do the things Jesus did?

What actions grieve the Holy Spirit? (See Eph. 4:30-32.)

What does it mean to quench the Holy Spirit? (See 1 Thess. 5:19.)

How do you feel about the implications of John 14:12?

Questions, Questions

Jesus was in the upper room with His disciples celebrating Passover, instituting what we call the last supper with them. He told them that He was going away (Jn. 13:33). That statement prompted the disciples to ask Jesus a series of questions. In John 13:36, Peter asked, *Where are you going?* In John 13:37, Peter followed up with another question, *Lord, why can't I follow you now?* In John 14:5, Thomas asked Him, *If we don't know where you're going, how can we know the way?* Philip asked another question, or, actually made a request of Jesus—*Lord, shew us the Father, and it will satisfy us* (Jn. 14:8).

In response to Philip, Jesus stated that whoever had seen Him had seen the Father. Jesus went on to say that the Father spoke and worked through Him (v.10). He did not claim to do the things He did on His own—the Father worked through Him. Then He made the astounding statement that what He did, those who believe in Him shall do—and even greater things.

Seldom is John 14:12 ever addressed in most Christian circles. When it is, the tack taken to explain the meaning of the verse concerns the scale of our institutional ministries such as schools, hospitals, evangelistic, and mission endeavors. It is difficult to get around the fact that Jesus said *he that believeth on me* will do the things He did—even greater things. In His statement, Jesus focused on individuals, not on institutions.

Interestingly, Jesus followed His astounding statement of John 14:12 with teachings about the ministry of the Holy Spirit in believers' lives. The key to us doing what Jesus did is our relationship to the Spirit, to Jesus, and to the Father. In our own power, we can do nothing (Jn. 15:5).

One of the more revealing passages about the work of the Holy Spirit in the life of Jesus (and in ours) is in Matthew 12:28. Jesus had been accused by the Pharisees of casting out demons by the power of Beelzebub (Mt. 12:24). Jesus said that He cast out demons by the Spirit of God. This passage is extremely revealing about how Jesus lived His life and performed His ministry.

Being Human or Human Being?

Jesus lived His life out of His humanity and not out of His divinity. Paul emphasized this to the Philippians when he wrote in 2:7 that Jesus *made himself nothing* (NIV). The word is translated variously in various versions:

- *but emptied himself, by taking the form of a servant, being born in the likeness of men* (English Standard Version).
- *But made himself of no reputation, and took upon him the form of a servant, and was made in the likeness of men* (KJV).

The word that is translated in these ways is *ekenosen*. This is a compound word from *ek–* out and *kenoo–* to empty. The word has been subject to the speculation of theologians who have tried to figure out how Jesus lived His life. The position of church councils and theologians is that Jesus had two natures in one being. The term for this position is *hypostasis.*[1] The question that has occupied much debate over the centuries is how did these two natures relate?

We might be better served to see what the Bible stated about the manner in which Jesus lived. The words of Jesus serve us well here, *Search the scriptures; for in them ye think ye have eternal life: and they are they which testify of me* (John 5:39 KJV). Our best source for truth and insight is the Scriptures themselves. Here's what Paul stated about the manner in which Jesus lived.

In Philippians 2, Paul explained the relationship between *Logos* and Jesus, an integration of divinity and humanity. Dr. William Barclay said, "In many ways this passage is one of the greatest reaches of theological thought in the New Testament, but its aim was to persuade the Philippians to live a life in which disunity, discord, and personal ambition had no place."[2] These verses are crucial to comprehending what the *Logos* did, becoming a human being.

Three Essential Ideas

Three ideas merge to help us understand Philippians 2:5-11. The *first* insight is from Joseph Henry Thayer. Dr. Thayer rendered *ekenosen* (εκένωσεν, from *kenóo*, a verb) to mean laying aside, not just to empty or to make empty.[3] The *Logos* did more than empty Himself. What did He lay aside? Some hold that He laid aside His equality with God.

This position is problematic. If He laid aside His equality, did He become less than God? Making Him less than equal with the Father is heresy.

Morphe (μορφή, a noun) is translated <u>form</u>. *Morphe* indicates the intrinsic, essential nature or attributes of a thing or being. Because it is impossible for God to be anything less than divine, laying aside equality with God, hardly seems a likely meaning of the act of the *Logos* and of the passage.

The *second* insight is from J.B. Lightfoot. He stated that the *Logos* stripped Himself of the insignia of majesty. An insignia is a badge or emblem of office or rank.[4] Dr. Lightfoot explained, "He [the *Logos*] divested Himself, not of His Divine nature, for that is impossible, but of the glories, the prerogatives, of Deity. This He did by taking upon Him the form of a servant."[5]

In verses 7 and 8, Paul used *heauton* (ἑαυτον), translated <u>Him-</u>

self. The word, a reflexive pronoun, connotes He Himself: the agent acting and the one acted upon are the same person.[6] The meaning emphasizes that the emptying and humbling by our Lord was sovereign, voluntary, self-imposed.

Though having an equal rank with God, He divested Himself of the rights of that rank. The divesting was coincident with taking upon Himself the form (intrinsic, essential attributes) of a slave. The *Logos* did not lose any of His divinity. To His intrinsic nature of deity, He added the intrinsic nature of a slave. The verb having become (*genomenos*/γενόμενος, v. 8) in the likeness of men, according Dr. Lightfoot, "marks the assumption of the new upon the old."[7] The incarnation inseparably linked the Divine and the human in Jesus.

The *third* insight is from J.B. Phillips. His translation, *The New Testament in Modern English*, captures the essence of Philippians 2:6-7)—*For he, who had always been God by nature, did not cling to his prerogatives as God's equal, but stripped himself of all privilege by consenting to be a slave by nature and being born as mortal man.*[8] Note the two words prerogatives and privileges. Dr. Phillips stressed that the *Logos* did not cling to His prerogatives and that He stripped Himself of His privileges.

Jesus, while fully human and fully divine, laid aside His rank and privilege to live His life as we do in order to provide a model for us. He lived His life in a way to show us how life was meant to be lived and how it could be lived.

The way Jesus lived, empowered by the Spirit and indwelt by the Father, is the way God wants all of us to live. Following His statement in John 14:12 that what He did we are to do and even greater things, Jesus said that the Holy Spirit would come to live within us (Jn. 14:16-17), that He would come to us (Jn. 14:18), that the Father and He would make their abode within us (Jn. 14:23). God—Father, Son, and Spirit—has come to live in us and to work His work through us. The ministry is His, not ours. He simply wants to work through us as He worked through Jesus. He really is wanting our availability and not our ability.

What Jesus did, we are to do. The fact is most of the time we don't. Why? Is it because the things Jesus did are no longer possible? Is the power that flowed through Jesus no longer available? Or, is the explanation related more to our own lives?

The Key to the Miracles of Jesus

The key to Jesus' miracles was not His own power, but rather the Father working through Him. The Spirit's power was the source of His power. The Spirit is the source of our power too. Without the Spirit's empowerment, we can do nothing.

If we had the same kind of relationship that Jesus had with the Father, we would have the same degree of power that He had. The Spirit would be able to work through our lives just as He did through the life of Jesus. The very words of Jesus bring our lives into question. We grieve and quench the Spirit in our lives and His work through our lives is limited. We limit God by our disbelief and by our disobedience. What could we do if we were as pure and true as Jesus in our relationship to the Father? Think of the liberty, power and joy we would have in our lives!

Why are the gifts given?

The New Testament presents three purposes of spiritual gifts.

 **Read the following passages to see if you can identify those three purposes.**

Purpose 1: 1 Corinthians 14:5, 12, 26; Ephesians 4:16

Purpose 2: 1 Peter 4:10

Purpose 3: 1 Peter 4:11

The gifts are given

    -to build up the Body of Christ, the church

    -to minister to one another

    -to glorify God

To build up the church

Spiritual gifts are given to edify or build up the Body of Christ, the church. The church grows qualitatively and quantitatively—that is, spiritually and numerically. In 1 Corinthians 14:5,12,26—Paul stressed the edification (the building up) of the church.

This theme of edification or building up is repeated in Ephesians 4:16. In that passage, Paul uses the image of the body to emphasize that the Body (church) will be built up as each part performs its particular assignment.

The NIV states this clearly—*From Him the whole body, joined and held together by every supporting ligament, grows and builds itself up in love, as each part does its work* (Eph. 4:16). As we utilize our gifts in ministry, new believers will be brought to faith in Christ. As other believers teach and minister, the new believers will be developed or matured in their faith. The net effect is the church will be built up.

Often when we think of a church being "built up" the only dimension that comes to mind is numerical growth. What other ways can you imagine the church being built up?

To minister to one another

The Apostle Peter in his first epistle addressed the concept of spiritual gifts. In many ways, the letter is a "primer" for Christian living—addressing the basic issues of Christian living. In his first epistle, Peter writes—*As every man hath received the gift, even so minister the same one to another, as good stewards of the manifold grace of God* (1 Peter 4:10 KJV). Several key insights into spiritual gifts are gained from this verse.

Look at the following verse and make as many observations as you can about spiritual gifts: *As every man (person) hath received the gift, even so minister the same one to another, as good stewards of the manifold grace of God.*

49

For instance:
1. Every believer has a gift—no one is omitted.

Here are a few observations that can be made from this verse about spiritual gifts in believers' lives.

2. The word for gift is *charisma*—grace gift. The gifts are gifts of God's grace.
3. We are given the gifts to serve one another—the gifts are not egocentric. The focus is outward, not inward.
4. Our personal ministries are directly related to our grace gifts. Somewhere within the scope of our gift or gifts, we will find our personal ministry.
5. The gifts have a beneficial effect upon the person who possesses the gift. Each of us has great personal worth. God has invested a special treasure in us (2 Cor. 4:7).

6. Spiritual gifts allow us to partner with God. Through the Holy Spirit, we are the recipients of these special treasures. We each have a contribution to make.

7. A mutual interdependence is implied—ministry is a two-way street. This is clearly stated in 1 Corinthians 12:14-27. Need is implied. None of us is self-sufficient. We are to minister to one another the gifts we have been given.

8. We have been given the gifts by God—He is the source of gifts.

9. We are stewards of the grace of God—the gifts are merely an expression or manifestation of God's grace. The verse implies an accountability to God for the use of the gifts He has given to us. A steward is an *oikonomos*, a ruler of the house. Joseph was a steward in the household of his master, Potiphar (Gen. 39:1-4). Joseph was in charge of the household of Potiphar and as a steward, he was accountable to his master. Accountability as a steward is the primary point of the parable Jesus told of the three servants who were given a portion of their master's property in Matthew 25:14-30. These servants were given responsibility by their master and held accountable. God gives us gifts and He holds us accountable for their use.

The word Peter used for gift was *charisma*. He states that every believer has received a grace gift to be used in ministry to one another. Spiritual gifts equip believers for ministry. The ministry is both within and without the Body. In his statement, Peter focuses upon the ministry to one another. Dr. Findley Edge writes in *The Doctrine of the Laity*—

> If you are a Christian, you are gifted. The spiritual gift was not given to you primarily for your benefit or primarily for your enjoyment. Paul said the gifts are given for profiting (1 Cor. 12:7). Peter said the gifts are given to minister to each other (1 Pt. 4:10). Gifts are for the common good and ultimately for fulfilling God's purpose in the world. (*Doctrine of Laity*, p.105)

The ministry that achieves God's purpose in the world will not stop with a ministry to one another. In a teaching session of the *Doctrine of the Laity*, Dr. Edge stated that probably only 20% of the Body will find its ministry inside the church, within the four walls of the church. The rest, the other 80%, will find their ministry in the world. In the world is where we represent Christ to the vast majority of humankind.

To glorify God
The theme of gifts continues in 1 Peter 4:11 by providing some guidelines for using gifts—*If any person speak, let him speak as the oracles of God; if any man minister, let him do it as of the ability which God giveth: that God in all things may be glorified through Jesus Christ, to whom be praise and dominion for ever and ever. Amen.*

How does this verse compare to our definition of spiritual gifts? Remember it—*a gift is a supernatural ability given by grace empowering believers for service and displaying the presence of God in our lives.*

What does Peter state as a purpose of grace gifts in this verse?

To glorify God—what does it mean? The word Peter used that is translated glorified means to make renowned, render illustrious, that is, to cause the dignity and worth of some person or thing to become manifest and acknowledged (Thayer p.157). When a Christian uses his or her gift in ministry, God's worth and person are manifested to those who see the gift exercised or who are the recipients of the ben-

efits of the gift. Jesus referred to this in the Sermon on the Mount—
Let your light so shine before men, that they may see your good works, and glorify your Father which is in heaven (Mt. 5:16).

The basic meaning behind the word, *glory*, is a brightness, an effulgence, radiance, a shining forth. When we bring glory to God two things occur. First, He shines through our lives—we reflect His radiance. Second, when our lives reflect the light of God, the world sees God—we "shed light" on God so those around us can see Him.

Through the exercise of our gifts, the world receives the reflection of God's light and God is seen more clearly.

 **When you think of someone who glorifies God by the use of his or her gift or gifts, who is it? How do they glorify God?**

Purpose of Gifts

To continue the work of Christ...Jn. 14:12

He founded the church...Mt. 16:18
We are to build up the church...1 Cor. 14:5, 12, 26
He came as a servant...Mk. 10:45
We are to serve one another...1 Pt. 4:10
He glorified the Father...Jn. 17:1-4
We are to glorify God...1 Pt. 4:11

Are Gifts Valid Today?

Are gifts valid today? Consideration of 1 Corinthians 13:8-11 is crucial in answering this question.

8Charity never faileth: but whether there be prophecies, they shall fail; whether there be tongues, they shall cease; whether there be knowledge, it shall vanish away. 9For we know in part, and we prophesy in part. 10But when that which is perfect is come, then that which is in part shall be done away. 11When I was a child, I spake as a child, I understood as a child, I thought as a child: but when I became a man, I put away childish things. 12For now we see through a glass, darkly; but then face to face: now I know in part; but then shall I know even as also I am known. 13And now abideth faith, hope, charity, these three; but the greatest of these is charity.

This passage is pivotal to our understanding of the validity of spiritual gifts today. The focal point is the statement of the Apostle Paul in verse 8 where he declares that gifts, at least three—prophecy, tongues, and knowledge—shall cease. The question that must be answered is *when* will this happen? When will these gifts cease to be operable in the work and ministry of the church?

The focus of the issue narrows further to the interpretation of *teleion* in 1 Corinthians 13:10. This is where the question of *when* centers. The question is right there in the text: *But when that which is perfect is come, then that which is in part shall be done away.*

When we encounter denial of gifts in certain Christian circles, it is usually traced to two positions. One of those is a ***theological bias***. Some hold the position that the gifts are no longer valid because they have passed away, no longer required. And they base their position on an interpretation of this statement from Paul.

Teleion means...

Those who invalidate gifts in our time base their belief by interpreting *teleion* or *teleios* as meaning the Bible. The position usually taken by those opposing the use of gifts today is that gifts were valid as long as Scripture was in process, but now they are no longer valid. We now have the complete Bible. It is a perfect and complete revelation of God's work and will, therefore, gifts are no longer needed by the church.

Opportunity for clarification on this issue came my way over lunch with Dr. Jack Glaze, former professor at New Orleans Baptist Theological Seminary. I was serving a local church in Florida. Dr. Glaze had been invited to our church to lead our congregation in a concentrated week of Bible study. During that time, I was developing a study of spiritual gifts for our congregation. Our pastoral leadership team was seeking to move the congregation to a gifts-based approach to ministry.

One of the issues that had to be addressed in the study and implementation of a gifts-based ministry was the question of the validity of gifts today.

Over lunch, I asked Dr. Glaze for an interpretation of *teleion* in 1 Corinthians 13:10. That was the hinge-point for accurate understanding of the subject of validity. He interpreted *teleion* to be used in two ways. The word used by Paul meant either:

1) the coming of the Perfect One, Christ, at His second appearing.
2) it represented the final sanctification of the believer, that is, our state of Christ-like perfection. (This final sanctification will be brought about by one of two events. One is the second coming of Christ—see 1 John 3:2. The other is the death of the believer. Paul noted that to be absent from the body is to be present with the Lord—2 Corinthians 5:8.)

In either instance, gifts are still valid and operative in the lives of believers and the life of the church until those events take place.

Thayer's Greek lexicon defines *teleion* in this passage to mean the perfect state of all things to be ushered in at the second coming of Christ. One of the uses that Dr. Glaze suggested. Since Christ has not come yet, the gifts are still operative.

Now and Then

The validity of gifts is a **now** and *then* issue: *For **now** we see through a glass, darkly; but **then** face to face: **now** I know in part; but **then** shall I know even as also I am known* (1 Cor. 13:12).

The passage itself clarifies what Paul meant. *Now* obviously refers to the present; *then* refers to a future point. When *then* comes, we will see face to face and know as we are known. Obviously, this means when we see the Lord face to face (because of death or because Christ returns). At that point, we will no longer know in part, but we will know as fully as we are fully known. At that point, gifts no longer will be needed. Until then, the gifts—all the gifts—are valid.

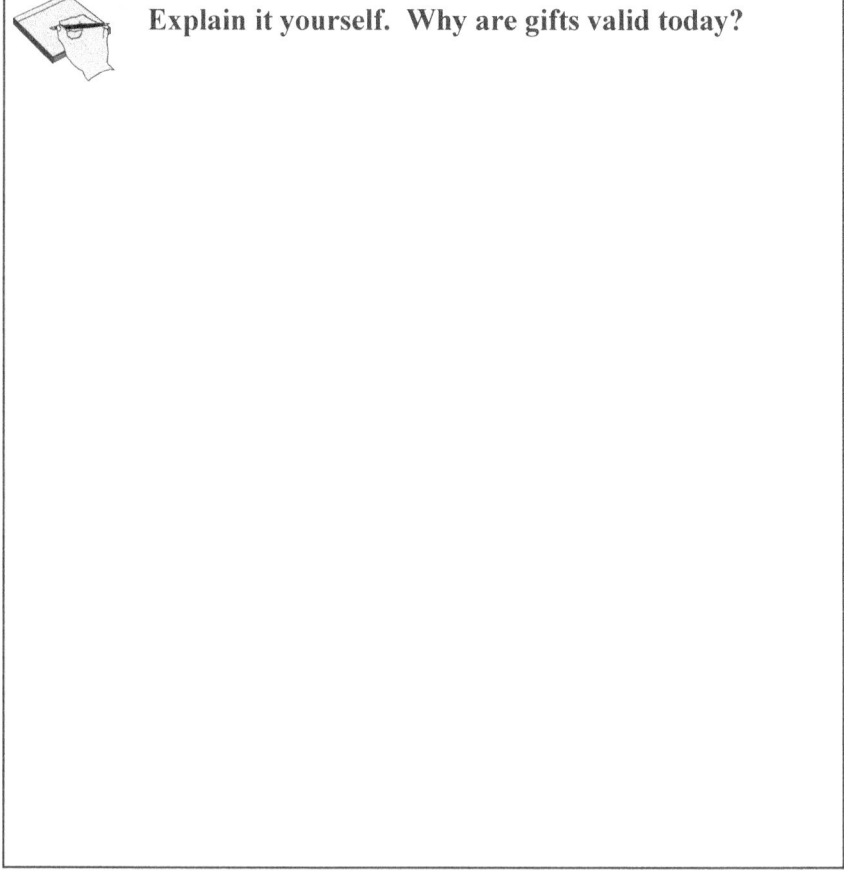

Explain it yourself. Why are gifts valid today?

The Second Bias

Let's not let this get lost. I mentioned earlier that when we encounter denial of gifts in certain Christian circles, it is usually traced to two positions. The first was the *theological bias*. These believe that the spiritual gifts became obsolete when the full revelation of Scripture had been given.

The second bias is an *experiential bias*. Some people, particularly those in church leadership positions, have had negative experiences of some kind with spiritual gifts. Usually the gifts have been abused in some manner resulting in a negative experience and a backlash against the use of spiritual gifts.

Earlier Dr. W.A. Criswell and his comment that tongues are of the devil was mentioned. That comment arose from negative experiences with the issue. His backlash was born of abuses some leaders and churches in his circle had experienced with the gifts of tongues specifically.

I encountered a similar reaction with an executive in the group who originally published this little workbook on spiritual gifts. One of the departments under this man's supervision was publishing the piece. My contact asked me to come to a meeting with this particular executive. They were vacillating on publishing the material because I had included all the gifts listed in the New Testament in Paul's writings. Of primary concern was tongues.

The group prided itself on holding that the Bible is *"the rule and guide in all matters of faith and practice."* So I brought a New Testament in my pocket. Entering the room, I laid it on the table.

As the discussion progressed, my defense for inclusion of the "sign" gifts—tongues, interpretation, healing, miracles—was that they were included in the New Testament. And that I could find no place in Scripture where any of these had been invalidated.

Further into the discussion, the executive revealed that he had a very negative experience in his church. A group of believers in the church he attended had become enthralled with the gift of tongues.

They were not acting in accord with the Scripture in their exercise of the gift. No interpretation. Demanding that all evidence this gift as a sign of their relationship with God. Eventually, a split occurred in the fellowship. Many left the congregation to create another assembly where they "had freedom to follow the leadership of the Spirit."

That experience was in the background of the executive's position on the inclusion of gifts that could prove problematic. This bias was experiential.

My position was biblical. You could call it my theological bias. If God said it, we could not remove it or ignore it. Just because some of the gifts were abused, we had no latitude to edit the Scripture. If we were to allow the Bible to be *"our rule and guide in all matter of faith and practice,"* we had to include all the gifts.

The executive was gracious and obedient to the Scripture. The book was published as written. But his concern is very real. Abuses of gifts can and do occur. The abuse should not prevent us from our own expression and obedience.

Notes and Observations

Session 4
What Are Some Difficulties
with Gifts?

In the late 1960's and early 70's a movement of God began to sweep across the United States. The "Jesus Movement" was part of that work of God as was the lay movement in the Methodist Church. Part of the movement was "charismatic" in the popular sense of the word. Salvation experiences, sometimes quite dramatic, were often accompanied by great exuberance and emotion. Worship services were very expressive. In some cases people spoke in tongues.

Some mainline churches made room for those who came to God in this movement and segments of the persons involved in the experiences found places in those churches. The major growth of the Assemblies of God and other Pentecostal-type churches is, in some ways, traceable to this period of time. These churches fit the experiences of persons coming out of this movement.

The established church, on the whole, was not prepared for the style of worship and the attendant phenomenon. Some leaders open-ly rejected the experiences. Some of those who did so were re-sponding to what they perceived as extreme and abusive practices. The dynamic of the Spirit's presence and particularly the gifts of the Spirit have always been open to abuse.

 **Read Acts 8:14-25. What was the nature of the abuse of Simon?**

What are some practices that you think would be called abuse?

Gifts and Abuse

Spiritual gifts seem to have always been ripe for abuse. The Corinthian church provides a prime example of a congregation who abused something God had given to equip them to do the ministry He had given them to do.

We have much for which to thank the Corinthian church. Without their abuses and misunderstandings, our own understanding of spiritual gifts would be woefully lacking. We might be making many of the same mistakes they did—as matter of fact, we have the letter written to them and we *are* still making the same mistakes!

The Abuses of Spiritual Gifts

Following are several abuses to which spiritual gifts have been subjected.

Confusing end and means

The gifts are never an end unto themselves. They are a means to an end—namely to build the Body, to minister to one another, and to glorify God. When we focus on the gifts alone, we confuse the purposes of God and abuse the gifts.

Glorifying the gift rather than the giver

God alone is worthy of glory and will not share His glory with another. The first of the ten commandments was directed at this problem—*Thou shalt not have any other gods before me*. The priority of God is not up for a vote. He will not abdicate His position. Some groups become so focused on the gifts and the accompanying experiences that they commit a form of idolatry.

Requiring everyone to possess the same gift

The Eastside Fellowship speaks in tongues—not just *some* of the members, but *all* of them speak in tongues. This congregation has taken a passage or two from the New Testament and made the experiences found in them normative to every Christian's experience. So adamant are they in this belief, if a person doesn't speak in tongues, the salvation of that person might actually be doubted.

The believers in the Eastside Fellowship have not taken into account the whole counsel of God. They have made a seemingly similar mistake to the Corinthian believers. From Paul's letter, we have the implication that the Corinthians, while they might not have *required* everyone to possess the same gift, seemed to believe that everyone could (and maybe should) possess the same gift. Paul addressed this idea of a universal gift—

Are all apostles? are all prophets? are all teachers? are all workers of miracles? Have all the gifts of healing? do all speak with tongues? do all interpret? —**1 Corinthians 12:29-30**

In the English text, the implication is clear from the rhetorical questions. No individual gift is possessed by all believers. The Greek text[1] is even clearer in the matter of universal possession of any particular gift. In the example that follows, note the small word ***μή***.

κυβερνήσεις, γένη γλωσσῶν. 29 μὴ πάντες ἀπόστολοι; μὴ
governments; kinds of tongues. [Are] all apostles?

πάντες προφῆται; μὴ πάντες διδάσκαλοι; μὴ πάντες δυνά-
all prophets? all teachers? [have] all works of

μεις; 30 μὴ πάντες χαρίσματα ἔχουσιν ἰαμάτων; μὴ πάντες
power? [2]all [3]gifts [1]have of healings? [2]all

γλώσσαις λαλοῦσιν; μὴ πάντες διερμηνεύουσιν; 31 Ζηλοῦτε
[1]do speak with tongues? [2]all [1]do interpret? [2]Be [3]emulous [4]of

δὲ τὰ χαρίσματα τὰ °κρείττονα·‖ καὶ ἔτι καθ᾽ ὑπερβολὴν
[1]but the [5]gifts [1]better, and yet [2]more [3]surpassing

ὁδὸν ὑμῖν δείκνυμι.
[1]a [4]way to you I shew.

This little word is a **negative** that Paul included so no mistake could be made by the Corinthians in his meaning. Instead of a series of questions, a series of statements might better help us understand

Paul's meaning. The passage would look like this:

All are not apostles! All are not prophets! All are not teachers! All are not workers of miracles! All have not the gifts of healing! All do not speak with tongues! All do not interpret!

One of the odd coincidences is that usually the gift that is the focus in congregations like the Eastside Fellowship is the gift of tongues. One of the probable causes for this is the statement in Acts 2:4, *And they were all filled with the Holy Ghost, and began to speak with other tongues as the Spirit gave them utterance.* From the experience of the day of Pentecost is built a whole practice in some churches of requiring everyone to speak in tongues as a sign of salvation or a sign of the "second blessing" (a term referring in some instances to the filling of the Holy Spirit or, as some others believe, the baptism of the Holy Spirit).

A valid argument could be made for evidencing any other gift as a sign of salvation. For instance, those possessing the gift of teaching might demand to see evidences of this gift from all other believers. Since virtually all persons speak, evidencing the gift of tongues is far easier than evidencing most of the other gifts. Paul is clear on this issue—no single gift is possessed by all believers.

 **What are some situations of which you are aware in which this problem might exist?**

Coveting another's gifts

Sometimes a person might not be satisfied with the gift or gifts which he or she possesses. They look at another person's gifts and wish they had those gifts. For instance, a person might have the gift of helps, a serving gift, that sometimes is vastly undervalued by a church that often elevates the speaking gifts of teaching or preaching. The attention and focus that falls on the speaking gifts might be coveted by the person without those gifts. Granted, this is not a mature response, but is one that occurs all too often.

Paul stated, *But now hath God set the members in the body, as it hath pleased him* (1 Cor. 12:18). When we despise the gift or gifts we have been given and covet the gifts of others, we are calling into question the wisdom and work of God. This reference is to God's design of our physical bodies. Paul is drawing an analogy between the physical body and the spiritual Body of Christ, the church. If God has designed the physical body, it stands to reason that the same design effort has gone into the church—universal and local.

Disdaining another's gifts

One of the major abuses practiced by the Corinthians was apparently a disdaining of the gifts of others. Paul seems to address this issue in the Corinthian letter—*And the eye cannot say unto the hand, I have not need of thee: nor again the head to the feet, I have no need of you* (1 Cor. 12:21). Apparently, some of the Corinthians were disdaining or disparaging the gifts of some of the other members of the church.

Paul emphasized the value of each member. He stressed the importance of every member of the Body as necessary to the proper functioning of the Body. Every part has a job to do. Sometimes the members of the Body that seem to be unimportant, are actually very important.

The eye cannot say to the hand, "I have no need of you," nor again the head to the feet, "I have no need of you." On the contrary, the parts of the body that seem to be weaker are indispensable, and on those parts of the body that we think less honorable we bestow the greater honor, and our unpresentable parts are treated with greater modesty, which our more presentable parts do not require. But God has so composed the body, giving greater honor to the part that lacked it, that there may be no division in the body, but that the members may have the same care for one another. If one member suffers, all suffer together; if one member is honored, all rejoice together (1 Corinthians 12:21-26 ESV).

 **Which gift do you think the members of your congregation would consider the least useful gift? Why?**

Using gifts for self-glorification

This abuse of gifts relates to the purpose of gifts to bring glory to God. When a gift is used for self-glorification, we are encroaching on the domain of God. This has similar effects as the prayers and alms that Jesus mentioned in the Sermon on the Mount—the prayer prayed on the street corner for the benefit of those who hear it, has received its reward; the alms given so that others might see, have their reward.

Causing disorder

At no time is God the author of confusion and disorder (1 Cor. 14:33). With this fundamental position, we must raise questions about the use of the gifts to create disharmony and disruption. In the Corinthian church, gifts, especially tongues, were being exercised in inappropriate ways in the public worship service. Paul specifically addressed this issue in 1 Corinthians 14.

The whole chapter deals with the problems being created in the public worship service by the abuse of the gifts—most specifically, the gift of tongues. In his treatment of the issue, Paul contrasts the gifts of prophecy and tongues. Toward the end of the passage, direct instructions are given that address the order that is to be maintained in public worship services.

What then shall we say, brothers? When you come together, everyone has a hymn, or a word of instruction, a revelation, a tongue, or an interpretation. All of these must be done for the strengthening of the church. If anyone speaks in a tongue, two—or at the most three—should speak, one at a time, and someone must interpret. If there is no interpreter, the speaker should keep quiet in the church and speak to himself and God. Two or three prophets should speak, and the others should weigh carefully what is said. And if a revelation comes to someone who is sitting down, the first speaker should stop. For you can all prophesy in turn so that everyone may be instructed and encouraged. The spirits of prophets are subject to the control of prophets. For God is not a God of disorder but of peace. As in all the congregations of the saints... (1 Corinthians 14:26-33 KJV).

 **What gift, or gifts, if manifested in your church, would cause the most confusion? Should these gifts be "squelched?" Why or why not?**

Making a gift a badge of spirituality

The tone of 1 Corinthians 12-14 gives the impression that a degree of pride was involved in the practice of spiritual gifts in the Corinthian church. In chapter 12, some of the members seemed to hold that the Body could function just as well without some of the members—*And the eye cannot say unto the hand, I have no need of thee: nor again the head to the feet, I have no need of you* (1 Cor. 12:21).

In chapter 13, Paul seems to reflect some of the possible

inappropriate behaviors of the Corinthians related to the practice of gifts. *Charity suffereth long, and is kind; charity envieth not; charity vaunteth not itself, is not puffed up* (1 Cor. 13:4). In chapter 14 some frictional actions between the members are intimated— *Brethren be not children in understanding; howbeit in malice be ye children, but in understanding be men* (1 Cor. 14:21). These statements give the impression that some of the Corinthians prided themselves in the particular gifts they possessed.

One can almost picture the exchange—one member speaks to another: *"Yes—I speak with tongues. I've had such a glorious experience with the Lord. Do you speak with tongues?.... No, well maybe you will some day."*

The badge of spirituality is experience. Some people wear it with a vengeance. Paul seems to take a swipe at these—*If any man think himself to be a prophet, or spiritual, let him acknowledge that the things that I write unto you are the commandments of the Lord* (1 Cor. 14:37). Since all the gifts are gifts of grace, we should all exhibit a deep humility, rather than a haughty pride.

Most of the abuses addressed to this point are easily recognized and usually disapproved or discouraged. Rejection of these practices will normally get a hearty "Amen" from many in mainline, traditional churches. Other abuses exist and are practiced far more broadly and regularly in these traditional churches than are the previous abuses in churches of different persuasions. Consider the following.

Denying the gifts

In the mid-1970's, many leaders in mainline churches openly denied the gifts. They were reacting to the abuses associated with the sweeping movement of revival that occurred in the late sixties and early seventies. The Jesus Movement we mentioned was one notable evidence of the revival. The intensity of the spiritual experiences were often accompanied by phenomena like those found in the early New Testament church—tongues, healing, and so forth.

This revival gained considerable notice and touched the lives of some in the mainline churches. As the experience of the revival spread, the practices such as speaking in tongues were brought into the churches of which these were members. Often, the churches and the leadership were unprepared, both by experience and theological position, to address these issues. In part this was due to a more rational approach to worship, study and religious practice found in these more traditional churches.

The approach many took was to deny the validity of spiritual gifts—in part or in whole.

One of the great tragedies is that to deny the gifts is to deny God's activity in and through the lives of believers. This limits the work of God only to the level of human activity, energy, and thought. The resulting work is impotent, mediocre, and restricted. The effect of the Spirit's power flowing through the early disciples was *awe* and *wonder* (Acts 2:43). Those seeing the effects knew they were witnessing something that was unexplainable apart from the hand of God. How long has it been since we have witnessed anything like that?

Remember the definition of spiritual gifts offered earlier? A spiritual gift is *a supernatural grace empowering believers for service and displaying the presence of God in our lives*. Every believer who exercises his or her spiritual gifts is displaying the presence and power of God. Instead of the extraordinary, this should be the ordinary expression of our lives.

Sometimes the argument is advanced that none of the gifts are operable at the current time. In most instances, passages from 1 Corinthians 13 are used to support the positions taken by persons who deny the validity of gifts today. Two positions are generally held— first, none of the gifts are operable today, and second, only some of the gifts are operable.

Those taking the position that none of the gifts are operable use 1 Corinthians 13:10 to justify their position—*But when that which is perfect is come, then that which is in part will be done away*. They interpret *teleion,* the word translated as *perfect* (KJV), to mean the Bible. Their stance is that when the Bible came, no more need existed for the gifts. This would be great if the word *teleion* meant the Bible, but it doesn't—as we saw. It means *the perfect state of all things to be ushered in at the second coming of Christ* or *the final sanctification of the believer* (that is, our state of Christ-like perfection) *ushered in by either the second coming of Christ or by death*. (Recall that this was presented in detail in the previous session.)

The second approach in denying gifts is to deny *selected gifts*. Those holding this position base their belief on 1 Corinthians 13:8— *Charity never faileth: but whether there be prophecies, they shall fail; whether there be tongues, they shall cease; whether there be knowledge, it shall vanish away*.

This position is a specific reaction to tongues. Tongues are problematic. They were for the Corinthian church—Paul wrote a large portion of his letter of 1 Corinthians about this issue. Tongues are problematic for many churches today. In some instances, tongues are a primary emphasis. The gift of tongues is a focus of much time, attention, and spiritual experience.

In other churches, tongues are absolutely denied and forbidden. Since tongues are one of the gifts specifically mentioned in 1 Corinthians 13:8, this verse is used to deny the existence of tongues today. This second position allows the existence of some gifts, while denying others—specifically tongues.

This position presents some problems. Since none of the lists in the New Testament are comprehensive (they appear to be representative of the whole concept of gifts), it seems that this brief list in 1 Corinthians 13:8 (prophesy, knowledge and tongues) is also merely representative. The position that these three specific gifts have passed away is untenable. Either all the gifts are viable or none are viable.

If these three representative gifts are invalid, all the gifts are invalid. If none are valid for today, then we are on our own to do the work of God—a discouraging thought! If it is a representative list, at some point all the gifts will cease to exist. When is that? It is when *teleion* comes—*when that which is perfect is come*. That has not yet come. At a future point and event, the gifts will no longer be valid. Until that time, the gifts, all the gifts, are valid.

For some people, the most acceptable list of gifts in the New Testament is the Romans list. The list contains seven gifts that are considered basic to the work of the church. It doesn't contain any of the *sign* gifts that present so many problems for some people. While this list fits the theological position of some regarding the sign gifts, the list must still be considered representative. Many who hold this list in Romans to be the only valid, operable gifts in the church today, neglect to notice that prophesy, in the Romans list is also one of the gifts in the 1 Corinthians 13:8 list that is destined to pass away—or, as some hold, has already ceased.

We must guard against merely taking a position (maybe because of the abuses we have seen) and imposing our framework or position on the Bible. The Bible needs to inform our theological position, rather than our theological position informing the Bible. The gifts are gifts of God's grace—evidences of His presence in our lives and the equipping for His work in the world—that are still valid today.

 **Have you heard someone deny the validity of any or all of the gifts today? If so, what was the basis of the denial?**

Neglecting one's gifts

Paul encouraged Timothy in his first letter—*neglect not the gift that is in thee, which was given thee by prophecy, with the laying on of hands by the presbytery* (1 Tim.4:14). One of the greatest abuses of spiritual gifts in practically every church is neglect. God has given the gifts to be used. They are not given to horde, admire, or brag about—they are given to fulfill God's purposes in and through our lives—His church.

"Use it or lose it" might be the slogan for this abuse. Actually, it is probably not lost (as in "I misplaced my gift and don't know where it is"). The image of the body is very instructive here. A muscle that is not used atrophies. Stan was in a terrible accident. He was hospitalized for months. He had to learn to walk all over again. His rehabilitation began slowly with small steps and small weights. His muscles were still there, they could be developed and retrained. This imagery is probably a more accurate understanding of the neglect of spiritual gifts.

[We have no scriptural basis for believing that a gift can be lost. We might say that the God who gave gifts in His sovereignty can re-move them by another sovereign act. While this is true, we really must say that in this instance, we have no direction and simply just do not know.]

One dimension of neglect that is often overlooked is the degree of absenteeism that afflicts our churches. How much of the Body is absent? Most churches have half of their members missing on any given Sunday. In all probability, those who are absent from church attendance are also absent from a church's ministry.

Churches have learned to function without all the Body being present. We have learned to adapt to much of the Body not contri-buting—but, all we are doing is "just getting along" in most cases. Paul emphasized the necessity of every member of the Body to the Ephesians—*From him the whole body, joined and held together by every supporting ligament, grows and builds itself up in love, as each part does its work* (4:16).

Wouldn't it be terrific if all the members of a church came together in one accord, in one place, filled with the Spirit (sounds vaguely familiar doesn't it)—why, we might have something like Pentecost happen again.

It is amazing that so many of the abuses committed in the New Testament are still being practiced in the church today. While abuses are committed, we should not let these abuses cause us to recoil from one of the most precious teachings of Scripture—**God is working through our lives to do His work in the world.** The gifts are gifts of grace equipping us for the various ministries we have been commissioned to do...*as my Father hath sent me, even so send I you* (John 20:21).

Which of the abuses do you consider to be the more damaging to the work of the church? Rank the abuses listed below. (1 = most damaging)

____Confusing end and means
     gifts

____Glorifying the gift rather
     than the Giver

____Coveting another's gifts

____Making a gift a badge of
     spirituality

____Denying the gifts

____Disdaining another's

____Causing disorder

____Requiring everyone to
     possess the same gift

____Using gifts for self-
     glorification

____Neglecting one's gifts

Guidelines for the Use of Gifts

The guidelines for using the gifts are related to the purposes of spiritual gifts and to the fruit of the Spirit.

Bring unity, not division

The gifts are given so that the Body would lack nothing and that no division would occur in the Body of Christ, the church.

But God has combined the members of the body and has given greater honor to the parts that lacked it,so that there should be no division in the body, but that its parts should have equal concern for each other. If one part suffers, every part suffers with it; if one part is honored, every part rejoices with it. Now you are the body of Christ, and each one of you is a part of it (1 Corinthians 12:25-27).

The emphasis on unity is a constant theme throughout the New Testament. For instance, the disciples were all in one place and in one accord on the Day of Pentecost. Paul stressed the unity of the Body in Ephesians 4: 3-6. While we have diversity within the Body members, we still form one Body.

One of the major concerns about spiritual gifts is that they have many times been divisive. Never is it God's intention that the gifts become a divisive issue. Just the opposite is true. The diversity of gifts are to equip the Body so it can become and act as a whole Body. While unity and function is God's desire, a church often frustrates the will of God in this. The Corinthians did this.

Look at Paul's words to them—*For ye are yet carnal: for whereas there is among you envying, and strife, and divisions, are ye not carnal, and walk as men* (1 Cor. 3:3)? If the length of lists and text are indicators, the Corinthians possessed more gifts than did any other church in the New Testament. Yet, the church is characterized as infantile and divided. Possession of spiritual gifts does not indicate spiritual maturity or unity. Paul laid the problem of division to their immaturity. When spiritual gifts create problems within a church today, spiritual immaturity is probably at the heart of the problem.

> **The Corinthians were—**
>
> **baptized in the Spirit (1 Cor. 12:13)**
> **gifted by the Spirit (1 Cor. 12:4-7)**
>
> **yet**
>
> **they are described as carnal**
> **and characterized by division, strife, envy**
> **(1 Cor. 3:1-4).**
>
> **Spiritual baptism + gifts ≠ maturity!**

The problem can reside both with those who exercise the gifts and with those who would deny or at least discourage the exercise of spiritual gifts.

One of the more difficult issues is tongues. Granted, in most instances, biblical guidelines are not followed. This alone creates difficulty—even division. For an example, let's make some allow-ances—let's allow that tongues are being practiced in accord with biblical guidelines—in both public and private worship. If tongues are being used under the biblical guidelines, the problem might not lie with those who are practicing tongues, but with those who have difficulty with those who are utilizing the gift of tongues.

God might be edifying individual believers (1 Cor. 14:4) or might have a message to edify the church (1 Cor. 14:5) or might be providing witness to the lost (1 Cor. 14:22). If we forbid the exercise of certain gifts with which we are uncomfortable (tongues or any other gift), we might possibly be hindering the work God is wanting to do in and through the Body.

On one hand, unless a gift is needed by a church, God probably will not give it. If a gift is going to create confusion or disruption in a congregation, God may not bestow that gift. Unity is God's objec-tive, not division. However, the other side of the issue is that if tongues are being used under the biblical guidelines, the problem might not lie with those who are practicing tongues, but with those who raise issue with the practice.

 **Does this thought have any implications for the existence of denominations?**

Build up, not tear down

The gifts are meant to be constructive and not destructive. Throughout Paul's directions in 1 Corinthians 14, he emphasized that the gifts are given to edify (build up) the church. **If one gift has weight over another, it has greater weight based on the ability of the gift to edify.** Note the following verses:

Follow the way of love and eagerly desire spiritual gifts, especially the gift of prophecy. For anyone who speaks in a tongue does not speak to men but to God. Indeed, no one understands him; he utters mysteries with his spirit. But everyone who prophesies speaks to men for their strengthening, encouragement and comfort. He who speaks in a tongue edifies himself, but he who prophesies edifies the church. I would like every one of you to speak in tongues, but I would rather have you prophesy. He who prophesies is greater than one who speaks in tongues, unless he interprets, so that the church may be edified (1 Corinthians 14:1-5).

So it is with you. Since you are eager to have spiritual gifts, try to excel in gifts that build up the church (1 Corinthians 14:12).

What then shall we say, brothers? When you come together, everyone has a hymn, or a word of instruction, a revelation, a tongue or an interpretation. All of these must be done for the strengthening of the church (1 Corinthians 14:26).

The gifts have been given to build up the church, not to tear it down. God is never pleased with anything that tears down the Body.

Accompany by fruit of the Spirit

Two connected subjects are mentioned in the New Testament that are often confused in the discussion of spiritual gifts—the gifts of the Spirit and the fruit of the Spirit. The gifts are grace gifts given by the Spirit, in part, to equip us for our ministry to one another. No individual has all the gifts. We have one or some of the gifts. We are interdependent upon one another for a total ministry in and through the Body.

While no one believer possesses all the gifts, we each should possess all the fruit of the Spirit. The fruit of the Spirit is the natural outgrowth of Christian graces produced by the Spirit's presence in our lives. Paul lists these in Galatians 5:22-23—*But the fruit of the Spirit is love, joy, peace, patience, kindness, goodness, faithfulness, gentleness and self-control. Against such things there is no law.* Paul went on to explain and to encourage the Galatians—*Those who belong to Christ Jesus have crucified the sinful nature with its passions and desires. Since we live by the Spirit, let us keep in step with the Spirit* (vv.24-25). If we *walk in the Spirit*, the natural product of the Spirit's presence will be the fruit of the Spirit.

When gifts of the Spirit are accompanied by the fruit of the Spirit, an individual and a church comes close to embodying Christ in the world. Many of the errors and abuses associated with spiritual gifts will be eliminated when the fruit of the Spirit accompanies the use of the gifts.

Use in ministry

God gives us the gifts to equip us to minister to one another. The use of gifts is a two-way street. We each have gifts within the Body. None of us is self-reliant or self-sufficient when it comes to spiritual gifts. As each person uses his or her spiritual gifts, a contribution will be made to the Body. Paul addressed the Corinthians—

The eye cannot say to the hand, "I don't need you!" And the head cannot say to the feet, "I don't need you!" On the contrary, those parts of the body that seem to be weaker are indispensable, and the parts that we think are less honorable we treat with special honor. And the parts that are unpresentable are treated with special modesty, while our presentable parts need no special treatment. But God has combined the members of the body and has given greater honor to the parts that lacked it, so that there should be no division in the body, but that its parts should have equal concern for each other. If one part suffers, every part suffers with it; if one part is honored, every part rejoices with it (1 Corinthians 12:21-26).

We are vitally connected to one another. The gifts we each have are not given for our own benefit, but for the benefit of others. Peter reminded his readers that the gifts were of grace and that we who have received them have a stewardship unto God for their use— *Each one should use whatever gift he has received to serve others, faithfully administering God's grace in its various forms* (1 Pt. 4:10).

 **In light of this, how do we explain church "splits?" Do you believe a split is part of God's will for His Body?**

Glorify God

When we act in accordance to the character of God, we glorify God —we reflect His nature to the world. When people see God's glory reflected in our lives, they are drawn to God. The exercise of spiritual gifts manifests (reveals) the glory of God. Remember, one facet of the definition of spiritual gift in this study is *phanerosis*, a revealing. The Spirit's work through our lives exalts Christ and glorifies the Father. The gifts are a manifestation (revealing) of God's presence in our lives. The use of the gifts is to bring glory to God.

In His priestly prayer (John 17), Jesus provides great insight into how we are to glorify God—

I have brought you glory on earth by completing the work you gave me to do (v.4).

All I have is yours, and all you have is mine. And glory has come to me through them (v.10).

For I gave them the words you gave me and they accepted them. They knew with certainty that I came from you, and they believed that you sent me (v.8).

As you sent me into the world, I have sent them into the world (v.18).

By His words and works, Jesus brought glory to the Father. He said and did nothing that was not given to Him first by the Father. Through Jesus, the world came to know something of what God was like. He said, *I have revealed you to those whom you gave me out of the world* (Jn. 17:6).

In all that He did and said Jesus was revealing the Father. He who is Light was shining forth through the life of Jesus—so much so that when asked to show the disciples the Father, Jesus said that if they had seen Him, they had seen the Father. John stated it like this in his prologue, *No one has ever seen God, but God the One and Only, who is at the Father's side, has made him known* (Jn. 1:18). Through Jesus, God was seen.

Jesus told His followers that they should let their light shine before men so that men might see their good works and glorify the Father in heaven (Mt. 5:16). As the Father sent Jesus, He sends us. As He glorified the Father, we are to glorify the Father.

God has given us the gifts of grace to equip us to do His work (He is actually doing His works through us). As we manifest God to the world in our work and words, as we utilize our gifts in ministry, God is receiving glory. Through us, as through Jesus, God is seen.

Rule by love

Most of the time that we read or hear quotations from 1 Corinthians 13, they are out of context. We can easily forget that the chapter deals with spiritual gifts. The chapter is located between a chapter laying the theological foundations for spiritual gifts and a chapter dealing with practical instructions related to spiritual gifts. Notice in the following passage how many spiritual gifts are mentioned.

If I speak in the tongues of men and of angels, but have not love, I am only a resounding gong or a clanging cymbal. If I have the gift of prophecy and can fathom all mysteries and all knowledge, and if I have a faith that can move mountains, but have not love, I am nothing. If I give all I possess to the poor and surrender my body to the flames, but have not love, I gain nothing (1 Cor. 13:1-3).

The Corinthians possessed many spiritual gifts. They practiced them actively. The were desirous of gifts. They abused the gifts.

Somehow they missed something very essential to spiritual gifts—they were not letting love rule. The ruling ethic for the use of spiritual gifts is love. The net contribution of a gift used without love is *nothing*! The royal law of love must rule if gifts are to have any contribution to the kingdom work.

Rank the guidelines for using gifts according to their importance to you. (1 = most important)

____Bring unity, not division   ____Use in ministry

____Build up, not tear down   ____Glorify God

____Accompany by fruit of the Spirit   ____Rule by love

Session 5
What Are The New Testament Gifts?

Several passages in the New Testament deal with spiritual gifts. The primary passages are found in the writings of Paul and Peter. Both men provide great insight into the operation of spiritual gifts in the lives of individual believers and in the life of the church.

In several of the passages, Paul provides us with lists of spiritual gifts. These are not meant to be definitive. They were used in his writings to the early churches to help them understand how God works in and through us as His children and as His church.

The passages Paul included are in his letters to the churches in Rome, Corinth, and Ephesus. Although none of these passages are definitive, they are illustrative of the range of gifts that God given to the church. And to be a bit more pointed, God gives the gifts to in-dividual followers of Jesus. He calls us *members in particular*, meaning that we are individuals and as such, individually gifted for our personal ministries.

Yet, Paul also speaks of the gifts in the collective Body of Christ. As we each utilize our gifts, the church will achieve in the collective the ministry that God wants to accomplish through the church, both universal and local.

Lists Are Helpful
In discussions today, much is made of various lists of gifts. Some current writers use a list of nine gifts, others fourteen, others fifteen or sixteen. One recent study went to the other extreme and provided no list whatever—confusing the issue even more.

Depending upon the theological orientation, you can find those who focus primarily on the list of gifts in the Corinthian letter—

mostly because of the prominence of the gifts of tongues, healing and miracles. Others accept the list found in Romans. This list seems to be more acceptable simply because tongues, healing, and miracles are omitted. The gifts in Romans 7 have been identified as the "motivational" gifts. These seem to be less threatening and less problematic. This list provides something of a middle ground— while accepting the idea of gifts, the complications posed by the sign gifts are skirted.

The best list to use is the list in the New Testament.

 **What are the gifts in the New Testament? Make a chart of the gifts in the New Testament by looking at the various passages and listing under each the specific gifts you discover in each passage.**

Romans	1 Corinthians	Ephesians
12:6-8	7:7, 12:8-10, 28-30	4:11

The following chart lists the specific gifts mentioned by Paul in his letters.

Spiritual Gifts
The New Testament Lists

Romans 12	1 Corinthians 7 & 12	Ephesians 4:11
Prophecy v.6	Celibacy 7:7	Apostles
Ministry v.7	Wisdom 12:8	Prophets
Teaching v.7	Knowledge 12:8	Evangelists
Encouragement v.8	Faith 12:9	Pastors/Teachers
Giving v. 8	Healings 12:9, 28	
Administration v.8	Miracles 12:10, 28	
Mercy v. 8	Discernment 12:10	
	Tongues 12:10, 28	
	Interpretation 12:10, 30	
	Prophets 12:28, 29	
	Teaching 12:28, 29	
	Apostles 12:28, 29	
	Helps 12:28	
	Governments 12:28	

Examine the three lists above. Draw lines from one list to the other two lists to indicate gifts that appear in more than one list. Then, make at least two observations about gifts from these three lists. (You might make several—but make at least two.)

1.

2.

Drawing from Paul's writings, we can make a composite list of gifts. Many Christians have long accepted the Bible as our authority in matters of faith and practice. Since the Bible is authoritative, the New Testament list is adequate and acceptable.

One point of clarification needs to be made concerning the list of "gifts" in Ephesians. The list is not exactly a list of gifts, it is actually a list of *gifted persons*—leaders in the church. The list of leaders implies the various gifts that these leaders would need and possess for their ministries. For instance, a prophet would be expected to possess the gift of prophecy; an evangelist would be expected to possess the gift of evangelism. Let's get a bit of insight using the gift of evangelism. It will help understand more about Paul's message to the Ephesian Christians.

Gifted Evangelists

We discover from Scripture that some persons have spiritual gifts that equip them to do the ministry of evangelists (Eph. 4:11). Philip is described in just this way: *On the next day we departed and came to Caesarea, and we entered the house of Philip the evangelist, who was one of the seven, and stayed with him. 9He had four unmarried daughters, who prophesied* (Acts 21:8-9).

Philip, one of the seven chosen by the church in Jerusalem to solve the issue of distribution to widows in Acts 6, is called *the evangelist*. Upon the death of Stephen, persecution by the Jews broke out in Jerusalem. The church (all but the apostles) were scattered. Philip went to Samaria where God used him in an area-wide crusade (Acts 8).

Then God directed him to leave that work and go to Gaza where he would encounter the eunuch who was treasurer to Candace, queen of the Ethiopians. We might wonder at God directing Philip to leave such a fruitful ministry and go witness to one man—until we know the rest of the story. Today, one of the oldest expressions of Christian faith is the Ethiopian Coptic Church. We have to wonder if that church traces its roots back to a man in a chariot who was reading Isaiah 53 when a man named Philip hitched a ride. Philip was a gifted evangelist who could persuade people to encounter the Living Lord Jesus by faith. And our bonus is to know that he had four daughters who prophesied. A faithful, gifted family.

Billy Graham was such a man as Philip. Called to be an evangelist, his message was always simple and direct—God sent Jesus to die for sin; turn away from your sin; believe in Him; receive God's forgiveness and eternal life. So powerful was he in his preaching that one wag said, "He could stand and read a Maytag washer repair manual, sing five stanzas of *Just As I Am*, and 5,000 people would come to faith in Christ."

You probably know Billy Graham's name, but you probably do not know Hugo White's. This powerful evangelist didn't preach crusades. He worked in a factory. He was a gifted evangelist.

So effective was he in winning persons that he changed the culture of his work place. So many were won that attitudes changed, behaviors changed, language changed. So greatly did the work place change that the workers began leading a Bible study group at lunch. Beyond this session's material, you will never hear Hugo's name, but he, just like Billy Graham, is an effective evangelist.

And before we leave this window into the gift of evangelism— while all might not have the gift of evangelism, all believers are to be witnesses. Being a witness is not optional for a Christian. We are witnesses by virtue of our faith in Christ. If we are His, we are witnesses (Acts 1:8). We tell others what we have experienced. Our task is to be witnesses to Him. The result is God's work. But some in the church have the gift of evangelism. And this is indicated by the position of evangelist in the list of gifted leaders in Ephesians 4.

A composite list of gifts is at the end of this session. You might want to use that chart as a guide to further study of gifts of grace.

Observations

Several observations could be made. For instance, the repetition of prophecy and teaching could imply the importance of these two gifts to the church. At the same time, the occurrence of tongues only in the Corinthian list might imply the lack of importance attached to this particular gift. The length of the Corinthian list could reflect the difficulty the Corinthian church had with the issue of gifts. Consider this, each list is different. This could mean that no list is intended to be a complete list. The various gifts listed might be only representative of the broad spectrum of spiritual gifts.

The three lists are from letters to three different churches. The lists might represent the specific gifts known to be in those specific churches. The list from Romans is generally recognized as the most basic of the lists. Since Paul did not know the Roman church as intimately as the others, the gifts he mentioned are broad and general in nature.

Bigger than Our Box

Are these gifts the only ones? Is it possible that God can give gifts beyond these? First Peter 4:11 reminds us that God is the one who gives the gifts and Paul emphasized to the Corinthians that the gift of these spiritual gifts is the sovereign domain of the Holy Spirit (1 Cor. 12:11). God can give what He wishes to give, when He wishes to give them, as the need arises in the church. Remember, even in this, that God probably will not give a gift unless that gift is needed by the church to do the ministry that God has given it to do. The gifts are not for our purposes, but His—not for our glory, but His.

Our tendency is to limit God by our own conceptions—or misconceptions. Our mistake is to believe that we can understand God, fathom who He is. We think that we can put God in our box. It doesn't matter how big our "box" is, God is bigger than our box. In Job, the nature of God is stated through Zophar's questions—*Can you fathom the mysteries of God? Can you probe the limits of the*

Almighty (Job 11:7). Paul expressed the same truth in Romans— *O the depth of the riches both of the wisdom and knowledge of God! How unsearchable are his judgments, and his ways past finding out! For who hath known the mind of the Lord? or who hath been his counsellor* (Rms. 11:33-34)?

Our theology must simply allow the possibility that God can move beyond our understanding of gifts and even beyond the biblical listings of gifts. This is simply an affirmation of the sovereignty and the majesty of God. No book can contain all there is of God— not even the Bible as magnificent as it is. If the Bible could, God would not be God. [However, any revelation of God and His work will conform to what He has already revealed in His word. The Bible remains our rule and guide in matters of faith and practice— and one of the things it teaches is that God is sovereign.]

John's gospel gives us a bit of insight at this point—*Jesus did many other miraculous signs in the presence of his disciples, which are not recorded in this book* (John 20:30). The phrase, *in this book*, probably refers to no more than the book that John was writing.

The insight that is helpful to us is that God did not see fit to communicate to us everything that Jesus did—just those things that were necessary to bring us to light and life. The final verse in John's Gospel goes even further—*Jesus did many other things as well. If every one of them were written down, I suppose that even the whole world would not have room for the books that would be written* (Jn.21:25). God revealed everything that is necessary for us to know about Him to bring us to light and life and to give us direction in living that life.

Making the allowance for other gifts is not to say that other gifts are needed beyond those listed in the New Testament. It is merely to say that if God wanted to or if the church needed them, He could give additional gifts if and when He wished. In this, we are simply recognizing God to be God.

Get it? Let's see. In the following space write your own explanation of what you just read.

Which Gifts Are More Important?

Are some gifts more important than others? What do you think?

Look at the list of gifts on the next page. Make a list of the seven more important gifts (1 = most important). Be prepared to explain why you selected the ones you did and why you ranked them the way you did.

1._____ 2._____

3._____ 4._____

5._____ 6._____

7._____

Are some gifts more important than others? The short answer is probably. Paul seemed to imply this in his lists of gifts in 1 Corinthians 12. The greater weight seems to be given to gifts such as wisdom, knowledge, prophecy, and teaching while tongues and interpretation are relegated to the end of the lists (12:8-10, 28). Greater importance seems to be given to certain gifts because of their ability to edify the larger Body (1 Cor.14:1-5).

Categories of Spiritual Gifts

Sometimes it is helpful to approach a study of the gifts by categorizing the gifts. Generally, any categorizing is arbitrary to a great extent. Hints are found in the New Testament that might help define some categories. For instance, 1 Peter 4:11 suggests two groupings—*speaking* and *serving* gifts—*If anyone **speaks**, he should do it as one speaking the very words of God. If anyone **serves**, he should do it with the strength God provides, so that in all things God may be praised through Jesus Christ. To him be the glory and the power for ever and ever. Amen.*

Another category is suggested by Acts 2:43 and 1 Corinthians 14:22—**signs**. *Everyone was filled with awe, and many wonders and miraculous **signs** were done by the apostles* (Acts 2:43). Paul called tongues a sign to unbelievers: *Tongues, then, are a **sign**, not for believers but for unbelievers; prophecy, however, is for believers, not for unbelievers* (1 Cor. 14:22).

The following lists are our arbitrary categories of the gifts.

Speaking	*Serving*	*Signs*
Prophecy	Ministry	Miracles
Teaching	Giving	Tongues
Wisdom	Administration	Interpretation
Knowledge	Mercy	Healings
Evangelism	Faith	
Apostleship	Governments	

Helps
Discernment
Shepherding
Encouragement

The gifts placed under *speaking* are gifts that are used primarily in proclamation. The gifts listed under *serving* equip the church to be more effective in expressing the caring, compassionate ministry of Christ. The *sign* gifts evoke awe and wonder from those who witness them. They are tangible evidences of the activity God in the lives of people—a witness that the kingdom has come in a dramatic new way (Mt. 12:28).

This grouping of the gifts is entirely arbitrary. A good case could be made for some of the gifts being listed in another list as opposed to the one in which they are now listed. For instance, while encouragement could be listed under *serving*, it could just as well be listed under *speaking*.

 **Now that was our list—what's yours? How would you group the gifts?**

Following is the composite list of gifts from Paul's epistles.

The New Testament uses specific words for the gifts. The only exception is in 1 Corinthians 7:7 where celibacy is implied, but not specifically listed. The following chart provides the specific words used for the gifts.

Gift	Transliteration	Text
Prophecy/Prophet	προφητειαν	propheteian	Rm. 12:6, 1 Cor. 12:29 Eph. 4:11
Ministry/Service	διακονία	diakonia	Rm. 12:7
Teaching	διδάσκαλιά	didaskalia	Rm. 12:7 1 Cor. 12:29 Eph. 4:11
Encouragement	παρακλησίς	paraklesis	Rm. 12:8
Giving	μέταδιδους	metadidous	Rm. 12:8
Administration	προϊστάμενος	proistamenos	Rm. 12:8
Mercy	έλεων	eleon	Rm. 12:8
Celibacy	(derived from the context)		1 Cor. 7:7
Wisdom	σοφίας	sophias	1 Cor. 12:8
Knowledge	γνώσεως	gnoseos	1 Cor. 12:9
Faith	πίστις	pistis	1 Cor. 12:9
Healings	ίαμάτων	iamaton	1 Cor. 12:9 1 Cor. 12:28
Miracles	δυνάμεων	dunameon	1 Cor. 12:10 1 Cor. 12:28
Discernment	διακρίσεις	diakriseis	1 Cor. 12:10
Tongues	γλωσσων	glosson	1 Cor 12:10 1 Cor. 12:28
Interpretation	έρμηνεία	diermeneia	1 Cor. 12:10
Apostleship/Apostle	απόστολοι	apostoloi	1 Cor. 12:29 Eph. 4:11
Helps	αντιλήψεις	antilepseis	1 Cor. 12:28
Evangelism/Evangelist	εύαγγελιστάς	euaggelistas	Eph. 4:11
Shepherding/Pastor	ποιμέας	poimenas	Eph. 4:11
Governments	κυβερνήσεις	kuberneseis	1 Cor. 12:28

Are these the only gifts? Read 1 Corinthians 12:11. God is sovereign. If other gifts are required by the church, He can certainly give them. But these are the ones He *has* given. That is a good place begin—or end.

Notes and Observations

Session 6
What Are the Teachings on Tongues?

For weeks the friend had been inviting Chuck to attend the revival service. Chuck struggled with the decision. He had a great relationship with his friend and didn't want to disappoint him. The problem was that Chuck was "Baptist-to-the-bone" and his friend attended Lakeshore Assembly. Chuck had heard that things got a little wild down at this church.

Finally, he agreed to go. The people were friendly and Chuck began to feel a bit more relaxed. That lasted until the pastor came to lead the congregation in prayer. Chuck bowed his head and nearly jumped out of his skin when the whole congregation began praying aloud at the same time. Some of the people were obviously praying in tongues. During the preaching, the evangelist would utter a strange language occasionally.

When the invitation came, several people went forward. Some had hands laid on them. Some spoke aloud in tongues. The evangelist approached Chuck, "Brother do you want the gift?" Chuck didn't know what to say. The only thing he could think of was Paul urging the Corinthians to desire the best gifts. Chuck looked up and said, "Thanks, but I'd rather have the better gifts." Then, it was the evangelist's turn to hardly know what to say.

Tongues give many people problems. Churches have split over the issue. Friendships have been strained. Confusion exists over the validity of this gift. Some groups practice tongues openly. Others do some theological gymnastics to argue against the practice.

We may take a degree of comfort in knowing that we are not the only ones to have faced these issues. The church at Corinth also faced them.

Important Instructions to the Corinthians

Paul not only provided lists of the gifts, he also provided much insight into their use and how they function in the church. We have the church at Corinth to thank for providing the catalyst for Paul's writing. First Corinthians 11:2-14:40 forms an entire section in Paul's letter. In this section he deals with problems in public worship: the veiling of women, the Lord's supper, and spiritual gifts.

The third topic, spiritual gifts, covers the largest section—12:1-14:40. These three chapters are dedicated to the issue of spiritual gifts and particularly to the problems the Corinthians were having with tongues. This section on spiritual gifts can be outlined generally by chapters. Note the following chart.

12	13	14
Theological basis for spiritual gifts.	Agape: the ruling ethic in the exercise of gifts.	Practical instructions on use of the gifts of prophecy and tongues

Read 1 Corinthians 12 and identify the theological foundations you discover in this chapter for the concept of spiritual gifts. Identify the verses from which the foundational concept comes.

Here's one to get you started:

1. We all have a gift or gifts. 7, 11

Here are a few that we discovered in the chapter:

2. All from same Spirit—vv.4, 11
3. They are for the common good—v.7
4. The many members form one Body—vv.12, 27
5. The Spirit creates the Body—v.13
6. All do not have the same gift and none has every gift—vv.4, 28-31
7. God places members in the Body as it pleases Him—v.18
8. Gifts are to work in harmony—vv.20-25
9. All are necessary for proper functioning of Body—vv.21-22
10. We are interdependent on one another—none is self-sufficient—v.25
11. We are connected in hurts and in joy—v.26
12. Some gifts have greater value to the Body—v.28

And this list is probably not exhaustive. You might have others.

But building upon this theological foundation, Paul provided the Corinthians with the general guideline of ruling all the gifts by love in chapter 13. He went on to address the specific issue of using tongues in public worship in chapter 14. It is interesting that the gift that gave the Corinthians the greatest problem, in many instances, gives churches today some of their major problems in the area of using spiritual gifts.

Teachings on Tongues

Tongues arouse some of the widest and most fervent responses in the Christian community. Some embrace the practice with exuberance—while others condemn the practice as being of Satan. Some see the experience as enhancing their worship and relationship to God. Some see the practice as disruptive and chaotic. Many simply do not know what to think or how to respond to the practice.

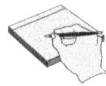 **Where are you at this point? On the following scale place an "X" to indicate your position.**

Believe in   Reject
the whole idea   tongues totally

|—————————————————————————————|

Why have you marked the scale as you did? Personal conviction; this is what you have been taught; this conforms with your personal experience; you just do not know what to believe. Probably if you said that you just don't know, you are right. Truth is, many wonderful, sincere Christians, some of them quite scholarly, don't know or disagree. Consider a few of the possibilities—

- ♦ tongues are a genuine, unknown, and "heavenly" language
- ♦ tongues are known languages like those spoken by the disciples at the Pentecost experience in Acts 2
- ♦ tongues are ecstatic utterances of individuals caught in the throes of exuberant worship
- ♦ tongues are a "prayer" language along the lines of the groanings of the Holy Spirit mentioned by Paul in Romans 8:26

No Simple Solution

The solution to this issue is not simply to "find out what the Bible says." That's actually part of the difficulty in this issue. The Scriptures are not exactly clear on this issue. (Now, if you are one of those people who have to have every "i" dotted and "t" crossed, this is going to be tough on you. A high degree of ambiguity is attached to this topic—just part of the turf.)

Consider some of these points—

- • Two different words are used by the New Testament writers when referring to tongues. One, *dialektos*, refers to specific known languages. The other, *glossa*, can mean the organ of the tongue or a language produced by the tongue.

- Paul brings prophecy and tongues into a direct comparison as to their relative value in the edification and the ministry of the church. He gives more weight to prophecy that edifies the whole church.

- Paul encourages the Corinthians to desire the gift of prophecy, but not to forbid anyone from speaking in tongues. The inference throughout the Corinthian correspondence is that tongues are not on the same level as many of the other gifts—especially prophecy.

- Tongues are not dealt with in the other passages about gifts in Paul's other writings. Only in the Corinthian letter do we find tongues mentioned, possibly because of the problems surrounding the gift in the Corinthian church.

- Paul might simply be making an allowance to the culture and the past pagan temple experience of the Corinthians. Not wanting to discourage these believers in their service and worship, Paul merely accommodated the practice and did not promote the experience—despite what some would make of the statement he made in 1 Corinthians 14:5—*I wish all of you spoke in tongues*. This flies in the face of what he had just written that we do not all possess the same gift.

See how confusing the issue becomes. This is not simple because of the biblical text. And it is further compounded by the particular theological and worship orientation of various groups or churches today.

 **Does your church have a specific position on tongues? Do you know how that position came about?**

Simply Known Languages?

The easiest and safest way of dealing with the issue is to treat the gift of tongues as known languages. The interpreter becomes simply a person who needs to be present who can make known to the congregation the message that is being spoken by the tongue speaker, a person who is speaking in a foreign language. Since tongues in the instance in Acts 2 were definite languages, we could easily make all the instances definite languages. This is a very rational and safe position—a position held by many wonderful Christians. This position, however, has some difficulties attached to it and most of them are textual.

Dr. J.W. MacGorman highlights from 1 Corinthians 14 some of the textual difficulties of understanding the gift to be simply foreign languages.

(1) It is addressed to God rather than to men. Those listening to the glossolalist cannot understand him, because he utters mysteries in the Spirit (v.2).

(2) The glossolalist himself does not understand what he is saying; thus he is urged to pray for the power to interpret (v.13).

(3) While speaking in tongues, one's mind and utterance are not coordinated as in ordinary speech: *For if I pray in a tongue, my spirit prays but my mind is unfruitful* (v. 14; cf. NEB: *If I use such language in my prayer, the Spirit in me prays, but my intellect lies fal-*

low.) Evidently in glossolalia there is a disengagement between rational processes and utterance.

(4) Glossolalia is a medium through which one may express praise or thanksgiving to God (vv. 16-17).

(5) The glossolalist is able to control the exercise of his gift. Otherwise Paul would not have commanded him to remain silent in church in the absence of an interpreter (v. 28). The exercise of this gift is not a seizure.

Upon the basis of these evidences we may conclude that glossolalia is Holy Spirit-inspired utterance that is unintelligible apart from interpretation, which itself is an attendant gift. It is a form of ecstatic utterance, a valid charismatic gift.

Dr. MacGorman makes the following conclusion about the experience of tongues (*glossolalia*) in the Corinthian experience— "Glossolalia is not speaking in foreign languages that one has never learned. The phenomenon of which Paul spoke had no vocabulary, recognizable grammar, and syntax through which thoughts were being communicated elsewhere in the world. In 1 Corinthians 14:2, the reason why no one understood what the glossolalist was saying was because he uttered 'mysteries in the Spirit,' not because no Tibetan was present!" [1]

Dr. MacGorman makes a convincing argument about the nature of the glossolalia that was experienced in the Corinthian church. This, however, is not the only tongues experience noted in the New Testament. The Pentecost experience in Acts 2 records that tongues were part of the phenomenon occurring in the body of disciples as a result of the Holy Spirit's indwelling, empowering and filling:

And when the day of Pentecost had come, they were all together in one place. And suddenly there came from heaven a noise like a violent, rushing wind, and it filled the whole house where they were sitting. And there appeared to them tongues as of fire distributing themselves, and they rested on each one of them. And they were all filled with the Holy Spirit and began to speak with other tongues, as the Spirit was giving them utterance (Acts 2:1-4).

This experience seems to be somewhat different from the experience of the Corinthian church. A different word is used in the text to describe the experience. *Dialektos* is the word used of the Pentecost experience—a word that is transliterated into English as <u>dialect, a language</u>.

Now there were Jews living in Jerusalem, devout men, from every nation under heaven. And when this sound occurred, the multitude came together, and were bewildered, because they were each hearing them speak in his own language. And they were amazed and marveled, saying, "Why, are not all these who are speaking Galileans? And how is it that we each hear them in our own language to which we were born (Acts 2:5-7)?"

The people in Jerusalem heard the sound like the rushing of a mighty wind. Drawn to the place where the disciples were, a crowd formed composed from Jews that had gathered in Jerusalem from countries all over the Roman world for the feast of Pentecost. The people in the crowd were amazed. They were hearing these others, Galileans all, speak in the specific *dialektos* of the various countries out of which these pilgrims had come. The disciples were speaking specific, known languages that they had not learned—that were given by the Holy Spirit for the communication of the good news.

Many who deny or oppose the ecstatic view of tongues make great use of the tongues experience of Pentecost. They refer specifically to the word, *dialektos*, to make their case that tongues, all tongues, are specific languages. However, the two other instances of tongues in Acts do not use *dialektos*. In the other instances (Acts 10:46 and 19:6) the word used for tongues is *glossa*. Therefore, it is unclear exactly what the experience was since *glossa* can indicate either a specific language or ecstatic utterance.

Glossa is used even in the Acts 2:4 where it is used to describe what was happening on the Day of Pentecost. While *glossa* is used of the experience, we know that experience involved specific languages and not merely ecstatic utterances because *dialektos* is used in Acts 2:8—*And how hear we every man in our own tongue (dialektos, language), wherein we were born?*

A case can be made for the experience in Cornelius' house (Acts 10) being similar to the experience of the disciples on Pentecost. Peter asked, *Can any man forbid water, that these should not be baptized, which have received the Holy Spirit as well as we?* (Acts 10:47). The implication can be drawn from his words that the experience was similar to the Pentecost experience—and that might mean that the tongues spoken at Cornelius' house were languages (*dialektos*) and not just ecstatic utterance. His meaning is a bit unclear because the specific word used in Acts 10 is *glossa* and not *dialektos*.

Not Either/Or but Both/And

Who's right—those who say that tongues are definite languages or those who say that tongues are an ecstatic utterance of an unknown, heavenly language? Actually they are both right. Tongues apparently are not an either/or issue, they are a both/and issue. In the New Testament, tongues are both a specific language and an ecstatic utterance. While this stance is not necessarily comfortable for some, it is biblical. Wherever we stand, let's stand there.

We might not understand the experience, the experience might not be within our personal range of experience, but it is a viable, valid spiritual gift. To deny it is to invalidate or to disparage a sovereign work of the Holy Spirit. Rather than simply taking a position, we and the kingdom might be better served to allow for the experience and take our approach to the experience from the Scripture. Paul had to deal with the issue with the Corinthians. Paul's advice on the matter might serve us as it did those first century Corinthians.

The same abuses and excesses in the Corinthian experience that caused Paul to write his guidelines to the Corinthians are the same aspects of tongues that cause people to recoil from the experience today. The advice Paul gave to the Corinthians for dealing with the tongues experience, therefore, stands well for us today. What were his guidelines?

Read Paul's instructions about tongues in 1 Corinthians 14 and list some of his specific guidelines here.

Practical Instructions

In chapter 14 Paul offered some practical instructions associated with the Corinthians use/abuse of spiritual gifts. Specifically, he contrasts prophecy and tongues. Note some of the following points he made related to the issue of tongues.

1. Prophecy (forthtelling) was given greater importance than tongues. Tongues, with interpretation, seemed to carry the same weight as prophecy. Prophecy edifies the whole Body (vv.1-5).

2. One purpose of gifts is to build up the church. Note Paul's emphasis in verses 5, 12, 26. (This building up includes both numerical and spiritual growth.)

3. Paul illustrated his points by use of musical instruments, the trumpet used to coordinate military movements and by use of a conversation with a person whose language one could not understand (vv. 7-11).

4. The Corinthians demonstrated their immaturity in their actions related to tongues (v.20).

5. Order was to be maintained in public worship. Tongues can be controlled just as prophecy can (vv. 27, 28).

6. Seemingly, women were actively participating in and promoting the use of tongues in public worship (34-35). Paul urged (possibly because of the pagan cultural practices) women to keep silent in the church. [This seems to be a localized admonition—remember Paul wrote of spiritual equality in Galatians 3:28, Philip had four daughters that prophesied (Acts 21:9), and Priscilla helped instruct Apollos in the faith (Acts 18:26). Paul had mentioned in his same letter to the Corinthians women praying and prophesying—the admonition was that they have their heads covered if they do. Paul may be giving a specific, practical application to the Corinthians.]

7. The Corinthians were not to forbid speaking in tongues, but they were urged to prophesy (v.39). Tongues were to be allowed in public worship only under the guidelines of verses 27 and 28.

8. Bottom line—everything was to be done decently and in order (v.40).

Paul included some practical guidelines for using the gift of tongues in this chapter. Compare the list you made on page 100 with the following list.

1. Whatever we do, do it so the church will be edified, built up (vv. 5, 12, 26).

2. If anyone speaks in a tongue, let that person pray that an interpretation would also be given (v. 13).

3. No more than three persons are to speak in tongues in public worship (v. 27).

4. Persons are to speak in sequence, not all at the same time (v.27).

5. Someone is to interpret (v.27).

6. If no interpreter is present, silence must be maintained in the public worship (v.28).

7. If no interpreter is present, the person may speak inwardly to himself and to God (v.28).

8. We are not to forbid speaking in tongues (v.39).

9. All things are to be done decently and in order (v.40).

All in all—it's not a bad list. If we followed Paul's guidelines, we might not have as much difficulty or confusion over this issue.

 Fred Vickers was uncomfortable. A friend had invited him to attend a revival service. The friend was a member of the Church of God. So life-long-Lutheran Vickers was a bit uncomfortable. Then a woman near the front stood and began speaking in strange words. Fred didn't know exactly what was being said, but he did know his Bible. He leaned over to his friend and asked when the interpreter would speak.

What biblical guideline did Fred reference?

Notes and Observations

Session 7

How Do Spiritual Gifts
Work in the Church?

The New Testament is filled with language images. These word
pictures are very effective in communicating a variety of important
concepts. For example, God is called a shepherd by the psalmist—
this teaches us that He cares for us in the same manner that a
shepherd cares for his flocks.

**List some of the images of the Church in the New
Testament and the lessons they teach.**

Image   *Lesson*

_____   _____

_____   _____

_____   _____

In the New Testament many images are used to help us understand
the Church. The Church is compared to an army, a bride, a building,
a flock, leaven, fire, branches, a family. Of all these teaching
images used to help us understand the nature and function of the
Church, the imagery of the human body is the most widely used
image in the New Testament.

The Body of Christ

The image of the body was extensively used by the Apostle Paul in his writings to the churches of the first century. Paul used this imagery extensively in Romans, 1 Corinthians, Ephesians and Colossians. The image of the body helps us understand several aspects of the Church.

The Structure of the Body

Christ is the Head; we are the Body (Col. 1:18). As Head of the Body, He controls the actions of His Body. He is Lord of life, directing the various members of the Body as they perform His will. Jesus controls and directs the work of the Church.

In our physical bodies, when we lift an arm, the muscles are merely responding to the impulses of the brain directing the muscles to contract. Similarly, Jesus controls the actions of the members of His Body, the Church.

Sometimes the brain is not in control of the body. Cathy was born with a RH-negative blood factor. She could not speak, although her mother could understand her needs. She could not walk or care for herself in any way. Her mother carried her to church until she was twelve, when Cathy became too large to handle. Cathy was a very special child, but sadly her body was not controlled by her mind. In a similar fashion, it is a sad when the Body of Christ, the Church, is not under the control of the Head— Christ.

 **What are some evidences that a church is *not* being controlled by its Head?**

106

The Function of the Body

Just as the human body is composed of many parts, so the Church is composed of many. Paul called the Corinthians the Body of Christ and members in particular (1 Corinthians 12:27). God has given each member of the human body a place in the body and a function to perform. He has done the same with the spiritual Body of Christ. He has given each member of the Body a function to perform. God equips the members of the Body with spiritual gifts. These spiritual gifts enable us to perform the tasks God has given. Several basic facts help us understand how God intends the church to function.

1. All members have gifts.

First Corinthians 12:7 and 11 emphasize that every person in the Body has a gift or gifts. We are all charismatic. We have been gifted by God for salvation and service. God never asks us to do a task without giving us the necessary resources to do that task.

2. All members do not have the same gifts.

Romans 12:6 reveals that we differ in our gifts by God's design and grace. The church is a well designed organism. Homogeneity is fine in milk but terrible in the church. Can you imagine how gross the body would be if it were all one part? Speaking of our differences Dr. Findley Edge has said, *"We must learn to celebrate our differences, not merely to tolerate them."* Praise God for the differences!

3. All members are placed in the Body by God.

God controls the church. At any given time and place, we are where we are by the will of God. We are gifted to serve in particular situations. God supplies members of the Body with the gifts they need to serve Him. God also supplies each expression of the Body with those gifted members it needs. This assures each local church that it has the essential resources to do the ministry God has for it.

4. All members are necessary for the Body to function as it should.

Paul emphasized to the Ephesian Christians the necessity of each part of the Body. The New International Version makes Paul's emphasis clear—*From him the whole body, joined and held together by every supporting ligament, grows and builds itself up in love, as each part does its work* (Ephesians 4:16). As each member contributes his or her ministry to the whole, the church will grow and be built up. To the degree that each member does not contribute to the whole, the church to that extent will fail to grow or to be built up.

Paul's image of the body in 1 Corinthians 12 vividly illustrated the necessity of each member to the body.

> *For the body is not one member, but many. If the foot shall say, because I am not the hand, I am not of the body; is it therefore not of the body? And if the ear shall say, because I am not the eye, I am not of the body; is it therefore not of the body? If the whole body were an eye, where were the hearing? If the whole were hearing, where were the smelling? But now hath God set the members every one of them in the body, as it hath pleased him. And if they were all one member, where were the body? But now are they many members, yet but one body. And the eye cannot say unto the hand, I have no need of thee; nor again the head to the feet, I have no need of you. Nay, much more those members of the body, which seem to be more feeble, are necessary: And those members of the body, which we think to be less honourable, upon these we bestow more abundant honour; and our uncomely parts have more abundant comeliness. For our comely parts have no need; but God hath tempered the body together, having given more abundant honour to that part which lacked: That there should be no*

schism in the body; but that the members should have the same
care one for another. And whether one member suffer, all the
members suffer with it; or one member be honoured, all the
members rejoice with it. Now ye are the body of Christ, and
members in particular.

—1 Corinthians 12:14-27

Ray Stedman has made a keen observation from this passage of
Scripture: the possession of spiritual gifts by every member and the
necessity of every member of the Body eliminates two mistaken
attitudes in the church—self-depreciation and self-sufficiency.

A. Self-depreciation

Some members believe themselves to be unnecessary to the Body.
They think their presence and participation to be unimportant.
Because they do not perform a certain task or do not possess a
certain gift they think they will not be missed. Yet Paul noted in 1
Corinthians 12:15-16 that just because one member is not like
another member it is no less a part of the Body.

Each member should accept his or her place in the Body,
believing it to be an important part—for it is. Our gifts and place in
the Body have been determined by God himself—*But now hath God
set the members every one of them in the body, as it hath pleased
him* (1 Corinthians 12:18). Who are we to criticize and disdain His
handiwork?

**Janet's frequent comment to anyone who would listen
was, "I can't teach or sing. I guess my role in church
is to just warm a pew."**

How would you respond to Janet?

B. Self-sufficiency

Some members believe they have no need of other members of the Body. They feel themselves to be totally adequate. This self-sufficient attitude is a mistake. God has made us dependent on others. Other members of the Body have gifts that contribute to our lives. We are actually interdependent. Fact is—we need one another. Paul voiced this interdependency in 1 Corinthians 12:21-22, *And the eye cannot say unto the hand, I have no need of thee: nor again the head to the feet, I have no need of you. Nay, much more those members of the body, which seem to be more feeble, are necessary.*

 **Gene is an adult Sunday School department director. His maxim is, "My way or the highway." A retired career military man, he was used to having his orders followed without question.**

How do you encourage Gene to be sensitive to those who work with him?

The Purpose of the Body

1. *The body makes a person visible to others.* We believe that a person consists of more than the physical. Within each person is a soul—an eternal, non-physical dimension of an individual. That dimension of a person relates to others through the medium of a physical body. The physical body helps us relate to our physical

world. In the same manner, the church is the visible Body of Christ in the world. Through us, Jesus relates to this world. While He was on earth, He had a physical body. The church, His followers have been indwelt by the Holy Spirit since the day of Pentecost. The Holy Spirit forms us into a Body—the Body of Christ (1 Corinthians 12:13). As the Body of Christ, we relate to our world. We make Christ visible to others around us. It is awesome to realize that all the people of the world will know of Jesus is what they see in the lives of the church.

2. *The body performs the will of the head.* The various functions of the human body are controlled by the head. The body's movements and functions are directed by the brain. The body gives expression to the will of the mind. As the Body of Christ, we are to be controlled by our Head—*And he is the head of the body, the church...*(Col. 1:18).

The church should express the will of Christ. Luke picked up this concept in Acts 1:1 when he describes his gospel account to Theophilus as the *former treatise...of all that Jesus began both to do and teach.* Luke's gospel was Volume 1, his account in Acts was Volume 2. The gospel recorded what Jesus **began** to do and teach. Acts was the continuing story of the ministry of the resurrected Jesus as He worked in and through the church by the indwelling power of the Holy Spirit. The early church continued the work of Christ—even as we do today. The church continues to express the will and work of the living Lord.

The Rainbow

The other image that has something significant to teach us about spiritual gifts is the image of a rainbow.

 **How many colors in a rainbow? 2   3   4   5   6**

Can you name them?

Actually a rainbow has three colors—red, yellow, and blue—the three primary colors. The six colors that make up the rainbows that we see in the sky are composed from those three primary colors. Red and yellow combine to make orange; yellow and blue combine to make green; and blue and red combine to make violet. (And yes, we do know about white, black, infrared, ultraviolet, and that light is actually a spectrum of light waves which cannot be combined—just a note to those of you who like to complicate a nice, simple, little illustration! And if a rainbow in the sky doesn't work—think of a child with crayons making a rain- bow on his or her art pad.)

Follow Your Rainbow…

The point that relates to spiritual gifts is that just as three simple colors can be combined to make the colors of a rainbow, the unique gifts an individual possess combine to create a unique ministry that contributes to the work of the church and the kingdom.

Think about the gifts in which you scored highest. The three, four, or five gifts that surfaced as strongest in your life "color" your rainbow—your giftedness. Within the range of those gifts you will find your special contribution and ministry.

112

Gifts/Body/Synergism

The combination of an individual's gifts equips him or her to make a unique contribution to kingdom ministry. The various gifts a person possesses sets up within that person a *synergy*. Synergy is *the cooperative action of individual agencies such that the total effect is greater than the two effects taken independently*. Well...that's what it is!

Now this is what it means—**the total is greater than the sum of the parts**. Synergy has a multiplying effect. In synergy 1+1=3. Like the rainbow example that has only three basic colors but can be made into six—that's synergy.

A person's combination of gifts has a greater effect than any one gift taken by itself. For instance, the gift of teaching combined with the gifts of knowledge and leadership prepares a person to be a more effective teacher. The ability to teach provides an effective avenue for using knowledge. The gift of leadership allows a platform for exercising the other two gifts.

This same effect is found in the Body as a whole. The individual members of the Body have a multiplying impact in ministry. Our individual ministries are complimentary to one another and contribute to the mission Christ has given us. When each part of the Body is functioning with the gifts God has given, a powerful effect is created. Paul noted the effect in his Ephesian letter—

> *From him the whole body, joined and held together by every supporting ligament, grows and builds itself up in love, as each part does its work* (4:16).

The effect of each part doing its work is that the Body grows and builds itself up in love.

We are interdependent, not independent. We must see our lives in relation to the other members of the Body. No individual has all the gifts necessary to perform the function of the whole. In the Body, interdependence creates a greater strength. The Old Testament states that where one can rout a thousand, two can rout ten-thousand (Dt. 32:30). The two relying on one another and God increase their strength.

Another image that shows strength from reliance is the image of a rope—*a cord of three strands is not quickly broken* (Ecc. 4:12). Where a single strand has a certain strength, when braided with additional strands, its strength is greater than the sum of the individual strands. Its strength is actually multiplied. This is synergism.

 **Synergism is a powerful concept for the church. Write a simple explanation of *synergy*.**

Explain how this concept relates to spiritual gifts and the church as the Body.

When we see ourselves as independent—as separate from one another—we set ourselves up for difficulties within the Body. Like a cancer within the Body, we become centered upon ourselves, our needs, our wants, our desires—even our gifts and our ministries.

Synergy not only allows for, but encourages differences. The greater the differences, the greater the strength. Plywood has great strength because of the different grained wood layers running in different directions. Each layer is very thin. By itself a layer is relatively weak. When glued with the grain of other layers running in all those different directions, its strength is multiplied.

Differences are built into the church by God. Just as He designed differences into the human body, He designed differences into the Body of Christ, the church. The Church was never intended to be a homogeneous body. Remember Paul's question to the Corinthians—*If the whole were an eye, where were the hearing?*

Homogenized milk is probably a good thing—but a homogenized church isn't. Our strength comes from our differences. Recall Dr. Findley Edge's comment. He was right when he said, "We must learn to celebrate our differences, not merely to tolerate them."

Within the combination of our individual grace gifts is the ministry that God has given each of us to do. Within the differences built into the church is the ministry that God has given each church to do. When we discover God's gifts in our individual lives and in the church as a whole, we find indicators or clues to the ministries God has given us to do.

Notes and Observations

Session 8
Where Can My Gifts Be Used?

Spiritual gifts have been given to us for use in the work God has given us to do. The gifts are not just for us to admire or show off. If we do not use the gifts in ministry, we frustrate the very purposes of God. To be more effective stewards of the grace God has entrusted to us, we need to discover, develop, and deploy our gifts in ministry.

Discovering Our Gifts

Gifts can be discovered in several ways.

1. Inventories

Several inventories are available to aid in the discovery of spiritual gifts. The one used in this study was developed by the Adult Section of the Discipleship Department of the Baptist Sunday School Board. Over a period of three years, thousands of participants helped refine this inventory to a 90 percentile range of accuracy.

The inventory is a series of statements that require a response. Point values are assigned by the participant to each statement. The statements have been developed around the spiritual gifts listed in the New Testament. The participant's responses to the statements indicate an area or areas of giftedness.

And just a word of counsel about inventories… As good as an inventory might be, it is still limited—by a variety of factors: the questions, the bias of the developer, the subjective nature of respondents. However, inventories are good in that they point us in the right direction. They eliminate some gifts and help narrow the range of exploration, helping us find the ministries to explore.

2. Identification by others

Other members of the church have an objective view of our ministry. Sometimes they may see a gift at work through our lives. The story of George Truett's call to the ministry is a prime illustration of others seeing one's ministry and identifying it. It was a deacon in a Saturday church conference who suggested that young George Truett be ordained to the gospel ministry. George then struggled with the decision for the balance of the day and evening, finally surrendering to the will of God and the church.

This man was called to pastor a church—to enter full time vocational Christian service—by a church that wanted him to be their pastor. He had no particular persuasion of a call from God until after the deacon proposed his ordination. He heeded the call, became a pastor, and ultimately left a stellar record as a preacher of the gospel and as pastor of First Baptist Church of Dallas, Texas—a church he pastored for 44 years.

An interesting activity that is sometimes done in groups studying spiritual gifts that know one another fairly well is to allow a time of sharing in which group members identify the gifts of others. Often the person is totally unaware that they are displaying any particular gift. They are just doing what comes naturally—or better yet, supernaturally.

3. In-service Experience

Persons can identify their gifts by taking on a variety of tasks in and through the church. Ministry in an area related to your spiritual gift will be easy and enjoyable. Jesus said the Holy Spirit would produce from within us *rivers of living water* (John 7:38-39). Ministry related to your giftedness will flow from you. If you struggle and strain to do a task, if it leaves you drained and down—odds are you are serving outside your gift. Experimenting with a variety of tasks and ministries can help identify your gifts. Mose Dangerfield said, "Our gifts are indicators of where God is wanting to use us."

Developing Our Gifts

Gifts can and should be developed. Paul urged Timothy to *neglect not the gift that is in thee* (1Tim. 4:14) and to *stir up the gift of God* (2 Tim. 1:6). Once we discover our gifts, we should give ourselves to developing the gift or gifts.

A reasonable question to ask is, Can gifts be developed? After all, God gives us these gifts of grace. Are we trying to improve on His handiwork?

Not to put too fine a point on the subject, *we are probably not talking of developing the gifts so much as we are developing our knowledge of the gifts, how and with whom they can be used, and developing the skills necessary to utilize the gifts to their fullest potential*. For instance, a person might have the gift of teaching. While the person might be a gifted communicator because of gift of teaching, skills in using teaching aids, techniques, and methods can be developed that make the gift of teaching so much more effective.

Development of gifts is done by three primary means.

1. Education

Gifts can be developed or sharpened through study. In the verses immed-iately following the one where Paul urged Timothy not to neglect his gift, he instructed Timothy to meditate and to give atten-tion to doctrine or teaching (1 Timothy 4:15-16). Study gives us a knowledge base from which we can work. Our study can acquaint us with facts about our gifts that can make us more effective in using our gifts in ministry.

2. Exercise

Another means of developing gifts is simply to use your gift in some kind of service. The old adage that experience is the best teacher applies here. At times it appears that we study and study and study, never applying the teachings we learn to life and labor. We keep gathering facts and knowledge, but never using them. It is similar to a body builder who studies physiology, anatomy, and nutrition continuously, but never lifts any weights. He knows all about the subject of body building, but he's not doing anything with the knowledge.

The most effective pattern of development might be to discover the gift, assign the person to a ministry, and then offer some type of training or education. The need for the education would be far more evident if the gift was being exercised in some kind of service.

3. Example

Example is one of the most powerful means available to those trying to develop the gifts of others. For instance, consider how parental examples are indelibly imprinted on the fabric of children. Traits, language, habits surface in the life of a growing child that can be traced to a parent's example.

Jesus recognized the power of example. He taught by example. Stressing the importance of service to one another, Jesus washed his disciples' feet at the last supper. When seated with them again, he said, *I've given you an example that you should do as I have done to you* (John 13:15).

Paul urged Timothy to be an example of the believers in his words, life-style, love, spirit, faith, and purity of life. Paul knew a good example was the best teaching model and personal witness for others.

A good means of developing a gift is to follow the example of another believer who possesses and uses that same gift in an effective manner. In trades of all types, apprenticeship is a valued means of developing skills and craftsmanship. An apprenticeship program in our churches could be an effective means of developing spiritual gifts.

Deploying Our Gifts

If spiritual gifts are never deployed in service, any study of gifts becomes a mere mental exercise in futility. **Gifts have been given to use.** If allowed to lie fallow, gifts fail to fulfill their God-given function. We have a stewardship of grace—*As every man hath received the gift, even so minister the same one to another, **as good stewards of the manifold grace of God*** (1 Peter 4:10).

As stewards, we will give an account to our Master of the way we used or abused the resources He has placed in our care. One day God will require us to account for what we have done with the entrustments He has given to us. Spiritual gifts have been given to us for use in ministry to one another. Within this purpose is the basis for our accountability.

Two arenas exist in which gifts should be deployed—one is the church, the other is the world.

1. Church
The church offers opportunities to utilize a wide range of gifts. Ministry within the structure of the church family calls for a variety of persons and gifts. A variety of needs engage believers in ministry to one another. The processes of Bible teaching, discipleship, missions, age-specific ministries like youth and children's ministry require people to serve as teachers, leaders, directors. Committees or teams give outlets for many believers to serve the church with their gifts. Worship services and outreach efforts engage other members' gifts. Support, care, and equipping ministries within the church family provide occasions to express our love for one another.

2. The World
Ministry, however, should not stop with our own. If it does, we will fail to use all the gifts God has given us. Dr. Findley Edge has long promoted the concept of lay ministry. He was a leading voice in the Renewal Movement that focused the church upon the mission and ministry of God. His voice in *The Greening of the Church* and *The Doctrine of the Laity* helped expand the work of God's people to

encompass all of God's people. He observes that only 20% of a church's membership is required to maintain the organizations of the church and conduct the ministry "within the walls of the church." The other 80% will find their arena of ministry in the world.

Every believer has his or her own "world." It is the sphere within which they operate. It includes their families, neighborhoods, circles of friends, business acquaintances. The great Quaker theologian, Dr. Elton Trueblood, has written that the vast majority of church members will find their ministry outside the church walls as *ministers of common life*.

He stated that the church suffered from segregation. The church is segregated:

- Geographically in that the church is the red brick building on the corner
- Temporally in that church is what happens one hour a week
- In personnel in that church is what we pay the clergy to do [1]

Church is the *ekklesia*, the people of God, the called out ones. Peter states this clearly in his first epistle: *But you are a chosen race, a royal priesthood, a holy nation, a people for his own possession, that you may proclaim the excellencies of him who called you out of darkness into his marvelous light. Once you were not a people, but now you are God's people; once you had not received mercy, but now you have received mercy* (2:9-10).

As the people of God, He equips us with these spiritual gifts, gifts of grace, that are the channels of God's power and work in the world. While some of us will find our ministry within the Body, the majority of us will find our ministry in the world. Our gifts will find expression of ministry daily in our families, communities, vocations or in specific ministry/mission projects.

Wherever we are, the church is. We are not bound by time, place, or space. And all are ministers because of the gifts God has placed in these earthen vessels. Let us be faithful stewards of grace.

Avenues for Using Gifts

The following is a partial list of ways we may express the spiritual gifts God has given us in service to the Body of Christ. No definitive list can be compiled—because God continues to create, and His people continue to imagine new ways to serve, teach, worship, and witness. The needs of the world evolve, and so do the avenues of ministry.

These suggestions are grouped under four primary callings of the church: **Serving**, **Teaching**, **Worshiping**, and **Witnessing**. Under each, we've noted the gifts commonly expressed in those areas.

1. Serving
(helps, mercy, giving, healing, governments, administration, ministry)

- Hospital visitation and patient care teams
- Crisis counseling and support groups
- Community outreach (housing, addiction recovery, mental health advocacy)
- Disaster relief and emergency response teams
- Church logistics and administration (personnel, finance, facilities)
- Technology and IT support for ministries
- Deacon ministry and care teams
- Meal preparation and hospitality
- Transportation ministry (shut-ins, seniors, youth events)
- Senior adult care and enrichment programs
- Foster and adoption ministry
- Grief support and funeral care
- Financial coaching and benevolence aid
- Special needs ministry
- Care for caregivers
- Volunteer coordination platforms (including online systems)
- Church security and safety teams

- Vocational mentorship and workforce readiness programs
- Day care, after-school programs, and parenting support
- Event planning and logistics (retreats, conferences, community fairs)

2. Teaching
(*wisdom, knowledge, teaching*)

- Bible study leadership (in-person and online)
- Discipleship group facilitation
- Digital content creation (podcasts, blogs, YouTube teaching)
- New believer and membership orientation
- Teaching ESL and literacy classes
- Curriculum development for all age groups
- Online course and devotional development
- Teacher training and leadership development
- Family and marriage enrichment classes
- Apologetics and worldview forums
- Hosting webinars or theological Q&A events
- Mentoring youth and emerging leaders
- Coaching for home school or Christian school educators
- Leading small group networks or neighborhood fellowships
- Theological writing and publishing
- Teaching in correctional facilities or recovery programs

3. Worshiping
(*prophecy, spiritual discernment, encouragement, shepherding*)

- Preaching and teaching ministries
- Worship leadership and music teams (choir, band, tech)
- Visual arts, graphic design, and stage decor for worship
- Drama and spoken word teams
- Prayer ministry leadership (intercessory teams, prayer chains, online prayer groups)
- Liturgical planning and service coordination

- Creative media (video storytelling, livestream coordination)
- Deacon service in ordinances (baptism, communion)
- Spiritual retreat planning and facilitation
- Worship service production (sound, lights, media projection)
- Digital worship support (captioning, accessibility, global broadcasts)
- Writing devotionals and liturgical prayers
- Prophetic encouragement and spiritual direction teams
- Organizing healing services or renewal weekends
- Hosting Christian growth conferences or seminar series

4. Witnessing
(faith, evangelism, apostleship, miracles, tongues, interpretation)

- Personal evangelism and testimony sharing
- Digital outreach through social media, blogs, and short videos
- Street ministry and community presence
- Campus and young adult ministry
- Cross-cultural and refugee outreach
- Evangelism training and mentoring
- Church planting and micro-church development
- Global missions and short-term mission teams
- Hosting seekers' dinners or open Q&A nights
- Discovery Bible Study, and similar platforms
- Ministry in correctional facilities or shelters
- Language-specific gospel presentations or interpretation
- Online prayer and outreach rooms
- Creative arts evangelism (music, dance, film)
- Evangelistic podcasting or livestream ministries
- Community service evangelism (faith in action projects)

 **What are some areas of ministry that you thought of while you were reading our lists? Take a moment and list them here.**

Burnout and Spiritual Gifts

Burnout is a word that has come into the vocabulary of corporate America in the last few years. It refers to a state of fatigue or exhaustion related to a particular job or task. The exhaustion is not necessarily physical—often it's mental, emotional, spiritual.

The condition of burnout is not unfamiliar to the Christian community. For years nominating committees of churches have sought to fill expanding organizational structures with the

Burnout:

State of fatigue or exhaustion related to a particular job or task.

workers available in the churches. They have used techniques ranging from tears to terrorism, greed to guilt, begging to berating—the slogan was "*a warm body in every slot.*" The results of this frantic activity to fill slots on organizational charts were burnout and dropout. The flight of workers from the ranks of the righteous compounded the problems for the faithful few.

The rule of thumb for church involvement has been—20% of the people do 80% of the work. This adage reflects a situation that promotes burnout and dropout. Another way of doing church does exist.

The image of the church as a Body found in much of Paul's writings illustrates a better way of "doing church." This image helps us understand that all members of the church have individual places of responsibility in the life and work of the church just as members of the physical body have their places. **God has already designed the church.** He has put the church together in such a way as to perform the mission He has for it to accomplish. *But now hath God set the members every one of them in the body, as it hath pleased him....but God hath tempered the body together, having given more abundant honour to that part which lacked: That there should be no schism in the body; but that the members should have the same care for one another* (1 Cor. 12:18, 24, 25).

Broadening the base of participation gives more people the opportunity to become involved and to contribute to the ministry of Christ through His church. A rule of thumb is *one person, one place*. Having one major task allows a person to concentrate energies and creativity on one job. The result is that the one job is generally done well. Time is allowed for a person to become involved in other aspects of life—like being a parent, a spouse, a worker. Burnout will be reduced. Persons will feel good about their contribution to the life of the church and to Christ's work. Joy in service will be a reality.

Burnout is related to spiritual gifts. It is an indicator that persons are serving outside of their gifts. When you are serving within the arena of your giftedness—power and joy will be evident. It will appear effortless to others and feel effortless to you. Jesus said that ***rivers of living water will flow from his followers*** (John 7:38-39). If you feel like you are pulling water from the bottom of a well, burnout is eminent.

Recently, a member who had pared back from three or four jobs to one said, "When I heard about this one job for one person, I thought it was crazy. I gave up some of my jobs. To my surprise, others stepped forward. I'm not doing as much, but I feel more effective. I don't dread coming to church—it's really a lot of fun."

Rivers of Living Water

Jesus said that the presence of the Holy Spirit would be a source of *living water*.

> *He that believeth on me, as the scripture hath said, out of his belly shall flow **rivers of living water**. (But this spake he of the Spirit, which they that believe on him should receive: for the Ghost was not yet given; because that Jesus was not yet glorified.)* —**John 7:38-39**

Living water is an image of contrast with water from a well. When water is drawn from a well, it takes work to get it out of the ground and work to get it to where it is needed. In contrast, the spring flows effortlessly to the surface with cool, fresh water. Remember the response of the woman at the well in John 4 when Jesus talked to her of *living water*—*Sir, give me this water so that I won't get thirsty and have to keep coming here to draw water*. As someone who came every day to draw water, she knew the value of *living water*.

In the panhandle of Florida is Emerald Springs, a large spring system covering almost an acre. Most of this system is gently bubbling up through the sandy bottom or filtering through porous, honey-comb limestone. This area is beautifully placid, but one part of the spring system rushes out of a deep gash in the ground, large enough to swallow a car.

Millions of gallons a day gushes from the spring. The force of the current is so great that swimmers cannot make headway against it. Getting into the mouth of the spring requires holding to rocks to keep from being swept away. Standing in the mouth of the spring, one feels the force of an endless supply of cool, clear, life-giving water. Such a contrast with drawing water from a well!

The Holy Spirit's presence in our lives produces a powerful, never-ending river of *living water*. When we are serving out of our giftedness, the Spirit flows through us—energizing our lives and ministries with power and joy. The difference in Spirit-empowered ministry and one driven by our own intellect and resources is the difference between a rushing spring of water and water drawn from a well.

God has chosen to work through believers by the spiritual gifts He gives. **Spiritual gifts are the *modus operandi* of ministry.** The power of God intersects the church and the world at the point of our spiritual gifts. When we discover our gifts and begin serving out of them the power of God flows through us to touch others and change lives.

Let the Living Water flow!

Don't wait to be asked. Pray for direction for your life and ministry. When God lays upon your heart a task or a ministry, share that with one of your ministry leaders. They coordinate the efforts and energies of your church. You can find encouragement, direction, and equipping for more effective service. They might know others who share a similar ministry concern with whom you can connect. Whatever you do, use your gift in service for God's glory.

To help you process your thoughts, complete the activity on page 129 page. Thoughtfully and prayerfully consider how God has gifted you for His service.

God equips each believer with gifts of grace. We are stewards accountable to Him for using our gifts in ministry. Serve in such a way that He may say to each of us, *Well done, good and faithful servant!*

Notes and Observations

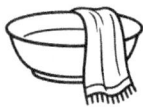 Gordon Cosby has identified three indicators of a call to ministry:

- ♦ You have a feeling of *Eureka*-I've found it!
- ♦ You see visions and dream dream.
- ♦ You can't stop talking about it.

What are your primary gifts? (Refer to page 22.) List the top five gifts here:

Do these best equip you for ministry in the church to the Body or through the Body to the world?

What are some of your natural talents?

What are some of the skills you have developed?

Do you have a particular passion for some avenue of ministry? What ministry creates excitement in you?

Your ministry will probably be found in the arena where all of these elements in your life converge. Look at your spiritual gifts, your talents, your skills, and your passion. Where are you equipped to serve in the Body? To what ministry do you feel God leading you?

Notes and Observations

Notes

Session 1

[1]*Spiritual Gifts Inventory* was developed by the Baptist Sunday School Board's Adult Section of the Discipleship Training Department over a three-year period (1983-1986) and is validated within a 90 percentile range of accuracy. Used by permission.

Session 2

[1]*Today's Parallel Greek-English New Testament*, (New York, The Iversen-Norman Associates, 1976), 487.

Session 3

[1]Hypostasis: a technical term in Christian theology employed in mainstream Christology to describe the union of Christ's humanity and divinity in one hypostasis, or individual personhood.

[2]William Barclay, *The Daily Bible Study Series*: *The Letters to the Philippians, Colossians, and Thessalonians*, (Philadelphia, the Westminster Press, 1959 edition), 47.

[3]*Greek-English Lexicon of the New Testament*, translated by Joseph Henry Thayer, D.D., (Grand Rapids, Michigan, Zondervan Publishing House, 1972), 344.

[4]J.B. Lightfoot, *Saint Paul's Epistle to the Philippians*, (London, Macmillian and Company, 1881), 112.

[5]Ibid

[6]Ibid

[7]Ibid

[8]J.B. Phillips, *The New Testament in Modern English*, (New York, The Macmillian Company, third printing, 1966).

Session 4

[1]*Today's Parallel Greek-English New Testament*, (New York, The Iversen-Norman Associates, 1976), 489.

Session 6

[1]J.W. MacGorman, *The Gifts of the Spirit*, (Nashville, Broadman Press, 1980), 42-43.

Session 8

[1]David Elton Trueblood, *The Company of the Committed*, (New York, Harper & Brothers, 1961), 9.

Get the companion book for pastors and deacons...

Developing Deacon-Led Ministry Teams

Developing Deacon-Led Ministry Teams is a practical and inspiring guide for churches seeking to reclaim the biblical model of deacon ministry. Moving beyond outdated structures and business-style boards, this book invites deacons to rediscover their calling as gifted servants—equipped by the Spirit and called to minister through the Body of Christ.

Grounded in Scripture and enriched with real-world application, the book explores:

· The evolving roles of deacons across church history

· The spiritual gifts that shape every believer's ministry

· Practical strategies for forming deacon-led ministry teams

· How to organize deacon service around calling—not obligation

Filled with insights, discussion points, and implementation tools, this resource is ideal for pastors, deacons, and church leaders committed to building churches that serve with joy, purpose, and power.

Because God didn't just call deacons to a title—He called them to a towel.

Available at Amazon, Barnes & Noble, and national retailers.

Coming Soon:

Reclaiming the Real Church

Rediscovering Identity.

Restoring Mission.

Reclaiming Our Calling.

In a time when many are questioning the direction and integrity of today's institutional church, *Reclaiming the Real Church* calls us back to the heartbeat of New Testament community. Built on a foundation of accessible theology, biblical models of leadership, and Spirit-empowered discipleship, this book examines what the church was meant to be—and what it can become again.

Drawing from decades of pastoral experience and collaborative insight, this study offers practical guidance for those longing to see the Church reformed, revived, and reengaged with its true mission. Whether you are a leader, a seeker, or someone who has grown disillusioned with organized religion, this is a call to reclaim what was never meant to be lost.

Companion resources include: Gifts of Grace and Developing Deacon-Led Ministry Teams.

www.ingramcontent.com/pod-product-compliance
Lightning Source LLC
Chambersburg PA
CBHW061651120626
46550CB00003B/904